DAVID WALKER'S APPEAL

DAVID WALKER'S

APPEAL,

IN FOUR ARTICLES;

TOGETHER WITH

A PREAMBLE,

TO THE

COLOURED CITIZENS OF THE WORLD,

BUT IN PARTICULAR, AND VERY EXPRESSLY, TO THOSE OF

THE UNITED STATES OF AMERICA

Revised edition with an Introduction by
SEAN WILENTZ

HILL AND WANG • NEW YORK
A division of Farrar, Straus and Giroux

Hill and Wang
A division of Farrar, Straus and Giroux
18 West 18th Street, New York 10011

Copyright © 1965 by Hill and Wang, Inc.
Introduction copyright © 1995 by Sean Wilentz
All rights reserved
Distributed in Canada by Douglas & McIntyre Ltd.
Printed in the United States of America
First edition published in 1965 by Hill and Wang
First revised edition, 1995

Library of Congress Cataloging-in-Publication Data
Walker, David, 1785–1830.
   David Walker's appeal, in four articles, together with a preamble, to the
coloured citizens of the world, but in particular, and very expressly, to
those of the United States of America. —Rev. ed. with an introduction /
by Sean Wilentz.
     p. cm.
   ISBN: 978-0-8090-1581-8 (alk. paper)
   1. Slavery—United States.   I. Title.

E446 .W15 1995
326'.0973—dc20

                                                          94045377

www.fsgbooks.com

CONTENTS

PAGE

INTRODUCTION. THE MYSTERIES OF DAVID WALKER   vii

PREAMBLE   I

ARTICLE I.   7
OUR WRETCHEDNESS IN CONSEQUENCE
OF SLAVERY

ARTICLE II.   19
OUR WRETCHEDNESS IN CONSEQUENCE
OF IGNORANCE

ARTICLE III.   35
OUR WRETCHEDNESS IN CONSEQUENCE
OF THE PREACHERS OF THE RELIGION
OF JESUS CHRIST

v

ARTICLE IV.   45

OUR WRETCHEDNESS IN CONSEQUENCE
OF THE COLONIZING PLAN

APPENDIX I. WALKER'S ADDRESS TO THE
MASSACHUSETTS GENERAL COLORED ASSOCIATION   79

APPENDIX II. EDWARD SMITH'S CONFESSION
OF SEDITION IN DISTRIBUTING COPIES OF THE *APPEAL*   85

SELECTED READING   89

INTRODUCTION

THE MYSTERIES OF DAVID WALKER

This was once a dangerous pamphlet. Published privately in Boston by its author, a black man, in the autumn of 1829, it delivered a furious indictment of American racism and slavery, coupled with a call to Southern blacks to rise up and overthrow their masters. The author's audacious message and his uncompromising style shocked white Americans. Even worse, the author found ways to get his words into the hands of his primary audience, "the coloured citizens" of the South. Within weeks of being printed, copies of the first edition were discovered circulating among the blacks of Savannah, Georgia. At about the same time, and over succeeding months, authorities seized additional copies in ports of call from Virginia to Louisiana. Legislators in Georgia and Louisiana became so alarmed that they enacted harsh new laws restricting black literacy, including a ban on the distribution of antislavery literature. (Similar legislation narrowly passed the Virginia House of Delegates but expired in the state senate; North Carolina enacted its own versions of the restrictions in the autumn of 1830.) Horrified Northern journalists joined in denouncing what a Boston editor called "one of the most wicked and inflammatory productions ever issued from the press." Even the antislavery spokesman William Lloyd Garrison, although impressed by the author's implacable hatred of slavery, found the pamphlet's "spirit and tendency" to be lamentably violent and provocative.

More than a century and a half later, David Walker's *Appeal to the Coloured Citizens of the World* is still a startling document. It certainly ranks among the angriest and most controversial American antislavery tracts. Addressed to Walker's fellow blacks, it is a powerful reminder that slaves and so-called "free persons of color" were important participants in the great struggle over slavery that led to the Civil War. Walker's withering attacks on racial injustice and his pleas for black unity anticipate lines of African-American protest that have endured among integrationists and black nationalists alike. Yet in many respects the *Appeal* is also a perplexing work, shrouded in mysteries that may never be fully solved. Who was David Walker? What shaped his thinking, apart from his sorrow and anger at the travails of his people? What did he think he would accomplish with his writing? And how did events reach a point where, for a brief but terrifying moment, his *Appeal* was the most notorious publication in America?

The known facts of Walker's early biography are sparse but suggestive. He was born in or near Wilmington, North Carolina, the son of a slave father and a free black mother (thus, under the laws of slavery, he was born free). The year of his birth is uncertain, although the most convincing recent research contends that it was about 1796 or 1797. By his own account in the *Appeal,* Walker left Wilmington as a literate young man and wandered around the United States, residing for an unspecified period in Charleston, South Carolina. In 1825, he turned up as a used-clothes dealer in Boston, where he would spend the rest of his abbreviated life.

Walker's decision to leave his hometown was not surprising. Although Wilmington was emerging as North Carolina's leading port, and although blacks greatly outnumbered whites, only a tiny number of the city's blacks were free. Slaves performed most of the city's skilled and unskilled work, leaving someone like Walker with meager economic prospects. Looking back on his life years later, Walker said nothing about Wilmington. Still, Walker's boyhood almost certainly contributed to his later preoccupations with religion and rebellion. At the beginning of the nineteenth century, the vast majority of Wilmington's blacks (along with a handful of whites) attended Sunday services at two local Methodist meeting houses, overseen by several African-American elders and stewards. Although it is impossible to ascertain whether Walker was raised as a church member, it is hard to believe that he grew up completely unaware of the Methodists' teachings.

Young Walker may also have learned about the history of slave unrest (and whites' fears of unrest) in the Wilmington area, which dated back to the years of the American Revolution. In 1775, amid rumors of an impending emancipation by British authorities, a slave conspiracy centered in Wilmington was detected at the last minute and suppressed. In 1781, when British forces under the command of Lord Cornwallis advanced toward the city, slaves flocked to the British lines in the hopes of gaining their freedom; they then assisted in the plunder of nearby farms and plantations, and stood by when the redcoats finally captured Wilmington and sacked it. Ten years later, news of the slave rebellion in Saint-Domingue stirred slaveholders' fears that their own slaves were plotting some sort of uprising; those fears materialized in Wilmington over the summer of 1795, when a band of runaway slaves under the command of a self-styled "General of the Swamps" terrorized local whites with sporadic violence. The attacks continued until local posses hunted down the rebels and killed them all, including their general.

Events in Charleston around the time that Walker lived there may also have sharpened his thinking about slavery, rebellion, and Christian righteousness. Over the decade before 1820—the period when Walker most likely left home—Charleston was something of a mecca for ambitious Southern free blacks. Unlike Wilmington, Charleston had a large free black adult population, which was employed in a wide range of skilled crafts as well as in petty retailing and day laborers' jobs. Many of the city's slaves, meanwhile, led relatively unregulated lives, hired out to work for local whites. Charleston's free blacks and slaves commingled in numerous formal and informal associations, including, after 1817, a formidable African Methodist Episcopal Church, organized in several congregations. As these black associations expanded, they struck some Charleston slaveholders as a potential threat to public order; these fears, in turn, led racial tensions to escalate. The tensions exploded in July 1822, when authorities uncovered the insurrectionary schemes of the ex-slave Charleston carpenter and Methodist church leader Denmark Vesey.

Along with the Richmond slave Gabriel's failed rebellion in 1800 and Nat Turner's Southampton uprising in 1831, Vesey's plot is remembered as one of the boldest slave conspiracies of the pre-Civil War decades. Its origins lay mainly among Charleston's African Methodists. The very existence of autonomous A.M.E. congregations unsettled white Charlestonians, who, with reason, became worried that black believers would seize upon troublesome scriptural texts about bondage and freedom and turn them into anti-slavery exhortations. After repeated warnings, local authorities tried to suppress the Methodist meetings, which only hardened the black Methodists' resolve to resist. A.M.E. church classes continued to meet semiclandestinely around the city. And in total secrecy from white Charlestonians, the redoubtable Vesey began recruiting a tightly knit group of prominent church members, along with an African-born conjurer named "Gullah" Jack, in an ambitious secret plan to raise a black army, seize the city arsenal, and lay Charleston to waste—after which the rebels would escape to freedom and leave emboldened plantation hands to rise up and destroy South Carolina slavery forever.

It was later reported that nine thousand slaves and free blacks from Charleston and nearby plantations joined the conspiracy (a number that was probably exaggerated). But no matter how large their army actually was, Vesey and his lieutenants certainly made ample and effective use of Biblical prophecies to inspire the troops, sometimes calling together Methodist class meetings as covers for their planning sessions. Moreover, Vesey's care in building a highly centralized underground organization successfully kept the plot under wraps until the very eve of the planned uprising. White officials learned of Vesey's plans only by chance; thereafter, in an atmosphere that sometimes verged on hysteria, they arrested and tried seventy-nine alleged conspirators, convicted fifty-nine of them, hanged thirty-four (including Vesey), and condemned thirty-five to exile (including some of those who had been acquitted).

None of the surviving sources on the Vesey affair mention anyone named David Walker. Neither do Walker's writings mention Vesey. There are passing references in the *Appeal* to Walker's Charleston days (see pages 12 and 39 below), including a description of a church camp meeting; the incidentals of those passages seem to date from 1821. The possibility that Walker was in the city a year later and the even more fascinating possibility that he was one of Vesey's unnamed foot soldiers will forever be matters of conjecture. It is

reasonable, however, to suppose that at some point during his time
in the small city he met people who were connected with the Charleston A.M.E. church, and who either knew or had known Vesey and
his confederates. In view of the heavy publicity given the affair
(including two book-length published reports on the conspiracy and
trials), it is likely that the literate Walker learned something of
Vesey's revolutionary blueprints. What is certain is that, seven years
later, Walker was mulling over an even more elaborate plan to
arouse the slaves of the South with Biblical prophecies of deliverance.

The record of Walker's Boston years is relatively full, although
it is not without additional mysteries. By resettling in the North,
Walker left behind scenes of slavery, but not of racial inequality.
Blacks—mainly petty shopkeepers and semiskilled workers and
their families—accounted for barely three percent of Boston's population in 1825. They faced numerous civil disabilities: Under Massachusetts law, blacks were barred from holding legislative office,
and from serving as constables or jurors. As in other Northern cities,
they also faced discrimination in a variety of public accommodations
and services, including, as Walker would note bitterly in the *Appeal,*
unequal schooling for their children. The city was not totally segregated, but black Bostonians tended to congregate in their own
enclaves, including a traditional black neighborhood near the North
End wharves and a newer one on the lower slopes of Beacon Hill.
Walker took up residence in the heart of the Beacon ·Hill black
district, and opened his used-clothes shop at the City Market; in
1828, he moved the shop to Brattle Street, closer to the wharves.
Even in his lowly occupation, he could count himself as better off
than many of the city's blacks—although, as we shall see, he may
have entered the used-clothes trade for reasons above and beyond
earning a livelihood.

Walker's business fared well enough that by the autumn of 1828
he was able to advertise regularly in a Boston newspaper. He also
got married and fathered a daughter. Less happily, he had a run-
in with the law in the spring of 1828, when he and two other clothing
dealers were indicted and tried for receiving stolen goods. All three,
as it happened, kept detailed records and were able to prove that
they had obtained the items in question on good faith. They rein-

forced their case by calling a number of character witnesses, including some whom the newspapers reported were "of the first standing in society." The experience of appearing before an all-white jury to pit his testimony against that of the police must have been unnerving to Walker. But as several friends and acquaintances later recalled, Walker was a willful man who was not easily intimidated, either in business or in his newfound role as an antislavery activist.

After his arrival in Boston, Walker had gravitated to prominent black residents who were engaged in various forms of antislavery work. Among his new friends were the hairdressers Walker Lewis and John Hilton, the Baptist minister Thomas Paul, and the tailor William Guion Nell. These men and others formed a kind of interlocking directorate of local black institutions that sustained the Boston black community and denounced both Northern discrimination and Southern slavery: Thomas Paul's African Baptist Church; the May Street black Methodist church (founded in 1818); the Prince Hall African Masonic Lodge (named after its founder, a Methodist minister who had served with the patriot army during the Revolution); and above all, beginning in 1826, a benevolent society called the Massachusetts General Colored Association. Walker, who joined the May Street congregation and rose to the secretaryship of the prestigious African Lodge, also became an MGCA stalwart. By the end of 1828, he had emerged as the most important black antislavery propagandist in Boston.

Walker's antislavery work was linked to that of two New York City free black agitators, John Russwurm and the Reverend Samuel Cornish. Over the winter of 1826–27, Russwurm and Cornish announced their intention to publish the nation's first African-American newspaper, which appeared in March 1827, under the title *Freedom's Journal*. Even before the first issue was printed, Walker held a meeting at his home with Hilton and Paul to drum up their support for the venture; thereafter, he and Paul served as the *Journal's* Boston agents. Over the coming months, Walker tirelessly supported the newspaper and its attacks on the American Colonization Society, the prominent white-led effort begun in 1816 that called for combining Negro emancipation with the removal of American blacks to Africa. When, in September 1828, Cornish abruptly resigned his co-editorship and Russwurm began a rapprochement with the colonizationists, Walker stayed loyal to the *Journal,* citing its paramount importance as an expression of unity and uplift for all colored people. (By the same token, after *Freedom's Journal* suspended publication in March 1829, Walker enthusiastically supported Cornish's short-lived anticolonizationist paper, *Rights of All.*)

Behind the scenes, Walker was in constant contact with other local activists, as well as with his associates in New York. And with his work for and occasional contributions to *Freedom's Journal,* he reached a far wider audience of Northern blacks. His most imposing public presentation prior to publishing the *Appeal* came in an address to the MGCA in December 1828, which the *Journal* soon published in its entirety (see Appendix I). It was an interesting performance, especially in light of what Walker would be writing over the months to come.

Walker's speech was a justification for the General Colored Association, a group he hoped and expected would become a national organization of America's half a million free blacks. Only by joining together, he argued, could those blacks who were free of slavery (but who were in truth, he remarked, only "about two thirds of the way free") improve life for themselves, their children, and the millions of their fellow blacks who were enslaved. Walker praised white antislavery men (including some who had endorsed the colonization line) for their sincere intentions, but he insisted that blacks could not stand by as "neutral spectators" of white antislavery efforts. Without going into details, he bid his listeners and readers to unite, to cooperate with their white friends in trying "every scheme that we think will have a tendency to facilitate our salvation," and to remain undeterred "from all lawful attempts to bring about the desired object."

Few, if any, members of the MGCA or readers of *Freedom's Journal* would have understood Walker's remarks as a plea to encourage slave insurrection. On the contrary, most Northern antislavery men, black and white, had pointedly discouraged talk of lawbreaking and violence, preferring moral suasion to physical force. But insurrectionary plans may have already been brewing in Walker's mind—plans that would not violate any Massachusetts law but that just might deal slavery a decisive blow.

How the plans took effect is the greatest mystery of all in Walker's

life. (Because Walker's antislavery activities never led to his arrest
or trial, he was able to take many of his organizing secrets to his
grave.) He certainly established some contacts with friendly antislavery Southerners who were in a position to help circulate
agitational literature. (Among these correspondents was a white
Milledgeville, Georgia, printer, E. H. Burritt, who was later apprehended with a twenty-copy consignment of Walker's *Appeal* and
a letter from Walker himself, confirming shipment of the pamphlets;
Walker also appears to have had some contacts among Southern
black preachers.) The most effective means of direct distribution,
however, was not through aboveground channels, but hand-to-hand
through the networks of sailors and ships' stewards that connected
Boston to the leading Southern ports.

These networks had long been a cause for concern, and not just
to Southern slaveholders. Over the late seventeenth and eighteenth
centuries, a distinct ocean-borne working class—what the historian
Marcus Rediker has called a "deep-sea proletariat"—arose on the
merchant vessels of the Atlantic world. With its mixed, international
ancestry, this working class forged bonds of familiarity and soli-
darity that cut across the ethnic and racial divisions of mainland
North America. Once ashore, it congregated in grog shops, sailors'
dives, and outfitters' stores at wharfside—rough, largely male pre-
serves that were well outside the pale of respectable society.

Notorious for its drunken rowdiness and sexual license, the sailors'
world was always suspect as a breeding ground of crime, above all
for the transfer of stolen goods. It was also suspect as a possible
breeding ground of sedition—the transfer of dangerous ideas. By
the 1820s, seaport Southerners were increasingly wary of the presence of black sailors in their midst, and of the disturbing influence
they might have on local slaves. (In the immediate aftermath of the
Vesey affair, for example, South Carolina officials passed legislation
that compelled Negro seamen to be incarcerated until their ships
left port.) But no degree of policing could prevent the circulation
of contraband (and dangerous writings) along the waterfront, and
from there to the hinterland.

It is unclear when, exactly, Walker struck upon the idea of using
his clothing business and his access to the sailors' world as a means
to spread his antislavery message. A white ship's steward, later
arrested in Charleston for distributing Walker's pamphlet, told au-

thorities that he was approached aboard ship in Boston by a well-dressed black man, who asked him to pass the copies to black Charlestonians—a fairly crude distribution scheme (see Appendix II). (It remains unclear whether the steward minimized his connection to Walker in order to allay his accusers.) But historians have suggested that Walker also took more elaborate smuggling measures. At his shop near the docks, sailors looked for cheap clothing (so-called slop goods) for their upcoming voyages; and Walker supplied them with used items, many of them obtained from other sailors, who had sold them to Walker for ready cash. It was a simple matter to collect batches of printed material, sew them into the linings of the clothing, and have them carried off undetected by sympathetic sailors bound for Wilmington, Charleston, Savannah, and New Orleans. Within days, copies of antislavery literature could be sent all across the South, spreading out from the ports along river routes to literate blacks who could relay the message to the slaves at large.

But what writings should be sent? Apart from some sermons, there was precious little in the way of published material by blacks intended for black audiences. *Freedom's Journal* contained useful commentary, but Walker wanted to provide a more extended account of slavery's causes and consequences than anything to be found in a newspaper. In February 1829, a mystical black writer, Robert Alexander Young, published a pamphlet in New York, *The Ethiopian Manifesto,* that prophesied the apocalyptic end of slavery and racial subjugation, and called upon blacks of all nations to unite—themes that Walker had in mind as well. But although Walker may well have been influenced by Young's work, he had ideas of his own about the curse of slavery and even stronger ideas on how to destroy it. In September 1829, he published the first edition of his own pamphlet and began sending copies southward. Two revised editions appeared over the next nine months.

The chief aim of Walker's *Appeal* was to inspire American blacks with a vision of hope and pride—and a prophecy of the destruction of the American status quo. As in his speech to the MGCA, Walker lamented the fatalism of so many slaves and free blacks—an attitude of resignation and servility that he blamed chiefly on white oppression, but one in which he believed blacks themselves were complicit.

Not only did black Americans submit to the lash and numerous subtler outrages; some were so hopeless that they willingly betrayed their braver brothers and sisters who chose to resist. It was time, Walker announced, to face up to the fact that "we Coloured People of these United States, are, the most wretched, degraded and abject set of beings that ever lived since the world began." Likewise, it was time for blacks to unite and fight back, in accordance with the word of God. But first they had to understand fully the depths of their degradation, and the various ways that white America kept them degraded.

The most obvious form of oppression was slavery itself, and the racism that whites invoked to justify it. Part of Walker's burden was to confront the racism forthrightly, and to ridicule its absurdities. Along the way, he added declarations of African racial pride, to offset the stigma attached to blackness that he had discovered everywhere he had traveled in the United States. "They [that is, the whites] think because they hold us in their infernal chains of slavery," he remarked, "that we wish to be white, or of their color—but they are dreadfully deceived—we wish to be just as it pleased our Creator to have made us. . . ." It was not enough, however, for Walker to discuss blacks' afflictions in abstract terms. To appreciate the gravity of the situation, blacks had to understand in detail how slavery and racism were essential features of America's supposedly egalitarian political and spiritual life. And so he turned to the writings of the most widely respected of American republicans, the recently deceased slaveholder Thomas Jefferson.

Walker did not choose Jefferson because he thought that the Virginian was unusually evil. He chose him because Jefferson was in so many respects an admirable man, the author of the Declaration of Independence and its ringing remarks about human equality—"one of as great characters as ever lived among the whites," Walker commented. And yet, Walker observed, even the great and influential Jefferson believed in whites' natural physical and intellectual superiority over blacks, beliefs that Jefferson had discussed at length in his *Notes on the State of Virginia*. To be sure, Jefferson had strong misgivings about slavery, which he had also expressed in his *Notes* (and which Walker slighted). But that was beside the point that Walker wanted to make. If Jefferson, the apostle of equality and the preeminent American *philosophe*, could write so emphatically about black inferiority, then it could be extrapolated that most white Americans held views that were at least as retrograde. Along with white avarice, it was those hateful views, Walker insisted, that were the major forces behind American slavery, and behind the political and civic inequality of free blacks.

The nation's white Christian churches, Walker continued, powerfully reinforced black oppression and submission. Some Christian clergy and laymen refused all religious instruction to the slaves. Others preached a corrupted Christianity that mingled blood and oppression with the Gospel, and justified black bondage. A few heroic black Christians (above all, Walker noted, the A.M.E. pioneer Richard Allen of Philadelphia) attempted to carry "the gladsome tidings of free and full salvation to the coloured people," only to meet with the opposition of tyrants and false Christians who feared that Christ's Word would arouse the wretched slaves. (Walker may have been recalling the troubles of Charleston's A.M.E. congregations.) Even in the North, white Christian clergymen showed little interest in evangelizing among blacks, and were content to preach in churches that strictly segregated white and black worshippers.

It is difficult to imagine a more thoroughly alienated view of the United States. For Walker, the sins of racism and slavery were so basic to American life that he sometimes sounded as if he were not himself an American—as if whites (about whom he had virtually nothing good to say in the *Appeal*) were Americans, but the sons and daughters of Africa were not. Yet even in his bitterest passages, Walker did not repudiate Christianity, republican principles, or his native country. In the fourth article of the *Appeal,* he launched an extended attack on the colonization movement, largely on the grounds that America's blacks were entitled to freedom and equality on their rightful soil, the land of their birth. Elsewhere, he offered a version of Christianity that was purged of racist heresies, one which held that God was a God of justice to all His creatures. In his final passages, he beckoned to Jefferson's own words in the Declaration of Independence as a model of equal rights, one that white Americans had desecrated with their murderous cruelties to blacks.

Hypocrisy with respect to equality was the chief American sin; and, Walker declared, God would not suffer that hypocrisy to con-

tinue. How, though, would it end? Walker held out the possibility
that white America, or at least most of white America, would feel
the moral pangs of its corruption and seek true Christian redemption
and racial reconciliation. ("What a happy country this will be," he
wrote, "if the whites will listen.") But Walker insisted that blacks
could not count on whites—their "natural enemies"—to have a
change of heart. Rather, blacks had to work on their own to speed
up emancipation and equality. More likely than not, that work
would lead to a bloody cataclysm.

It was Walker's prophecy of impending warfare and of slavery's
doom that most deeply shocked white Southerners and discomfited
Northern antislavery advocates. Walker was imprecise about how
his prediction would unfold. In the preamble to the *Appeal*, he
suggested that the slaves themselves might not lead the attack, but
that God would cause the whites "to rise up one against another
. . . with sword in hand." (In retrospect, these lines, written thirty
years before Southern secession, seem clairvoyant.) More often, he
envisioned a black uprising, or series of uprisings, that would slay
the oppressors—"root them out," in Walker's words. And in the
passages that Southern officials read with the utmost alarm, Walker
encouraged his audience to throw off the psychological weight of
servility and prepare to fight like men.

Walker proffered no details about how to wage an insurrection.
He did say that God would send a mighty general, like Hannibal,
to lead the forces of righteousness. (He may well have had someone
like the charismatic Vesey in mind.) But Walker wrote as God's
messenger, not as His strategist or field commander. The *Appeal*
was meant to clear the way, to pierce the fog of submissiveness that
Walker had discovered in his travels, to inform blacks of their proud
heritage stretching back centuries to Africa—to evangelize among
the lowly, as John the Baptist had evangelized, and to set their
sights on liberation and the coming of the Lord.

As a piece of writing, the *Appeal* captures the fascinating, at times
uneven voice of a self-taught man of letters. Walker had read widely
in secular as well as religious works, and he was not shy about
displaying his learning, as if he wanted to dispel by his very example
the myth of black inferiority. He was capable of making cogent,
off-hand references to the eighteenth-century British essayist Addison, to learned works of history, and to American legislative de-

bates, just as any well-educated white man could. At the same time, Walker's impassioned sermonizing, thick with Biblical allusions and punctuated with multiple exclamation points, occasionally lost the thread of its argument, perhaps because the author was composing and recomposing each edition hastily.

Still, with all of its quirks, the *Appeal* was (and remains) an arresting literary achievement. In a concise pamphlet—concise enough to be smuggled in batches inside a sailor's coat—Walker combined political argument, racial theorizing, historical reflection, and pre-millennial black Christianity in a stunning rebuke of the United States as he knew it. The result was a gripping call to resistance, one that was unsentimental in its appraisal of the toll that oppression had exacted from black America but that also insisted black Americans had the spiritual, intellectual, and physical resources to do God's will and secure their freedom. And over the winter of 1829–30, Walker busied himself sending wave upon wave of his call into the heart of the American Egypt.

Walker's efforts ended in a final mystery. In June 1830, he put a third edition of the *Appeal* through the press, defying the mounting outcries from Southerners and Northerners alike. The mayor of Savannah had written to Boston's Mayor Harrison Gray Otis, demanding that Walker be stopped; Otis, a crusty old Federalist, had replied that, although he abhorred the pamphlet, he was powerless to act, since no Massachusetts law had been broken. Soon after, Southern legislatures had begun passing new laws banning works like Walker's; and rumors had begun to circulate that Southerners had put out a price of $3,000 for Walker's head, a price that would rise to $10,000 if Walker were delivered to the South alive. Walker's friends pleaded with him to flee to Canada, but he refused. Then, on August 3, 1830, Walker suddenly died at his home. (His daughter had also died, days earlier, of lung fever.) No convincing evidence has ever come to light to show that Walker's death was unnatural. But many observers could not help concluding that he had been murdered.

No one picked up Walker's enterprise. Several of his distributors were arrested. And although fitful turbulence lay ahead (most famously Nat Turner's uprising a year later), Walker's writings brought no great insurrection. Yet Walker's improbable plot was not a total failure. At least one group of suspected conspirators—fittingly enough in North Carolina—was apprehended in 1830 with copies of the pamphlet. Additional copies were reported circulating among slave runaways and outliers as far away as New Orleans, and may have contributed to slave unrest. And in other ways, Walker's *Appeal* had a resounding impact on the politics of slavery and antislavery in the 1830s and 1840s.

In the South, for example, the appearance of the *Appeal* brought an important early step toward the consolidation of sectional white unity. Although slaveholders had long dominated Southern politics, white opinion on slavery before 1830 had never been monolithic. Backwoods areas, populated largely by non-slaveholding yeoman farmers, resented the power and prestige of the wealthier plantation districts, and were wary of new laws that seemed to entrench the slaveholders' command. These divisions resurfaced in some of the legislative debates that followed the discovery of Walker's *Appeal* (and, in Virginia, they proved great enough to defeat the proposed new laws on incendiary literature). In the long run, however, Southern alarm over Yankee propaganda and potential slave rebellion would help blur the divisions within the white South and reinforce intersectional antagonisms. The slaveholders' successes in clamping down on Walker and his accomplices in much of the South anticipated these developments. A full-fledged pro-slavery Southern nationalism, uniting white Southerners, was still only in formation in 1830—but the controversy over Walker's pamphlet certainly contributed to its emergence.

Walker's own words, as well as the Southern reactions to the *Appeal*, in turn stiffened Northern antislavery white opinion. Outside of the colonization movement and some religious sects such as the Quakers, white opposition to slavery was as yet a small current in Northern politics. Even the leading white antislavery voices, Benjamin Lundy and William Lloyd Garrison of the newspaper *The Genius of Universal Emancipation,* criticized Walker's pamphlet (Lundy more strongly than Garrison) for its menacing tone. Yet the Southern counterattack on Walker reinforced the impression among antislavery Northerners that slavery was tightening its grip on Southern (and American) politics. And Walker's bluntness helped persuade some Northerners, notably Garrison, that the fight against slavery and Northern racism had to be taken to a higher level. A

year after Walker's death, Garrison published in Boston the first
issue of a new paper, *The Liberator,* that would become the nation's
leading proponent of immediatist abolitionism, calling for an immediate commencement of black emancipation. Straightaway, Garrison reprinted most of Walker's *Appeal,* despite his earlier
disapproval. Over the following decade, tens of thousands of Northerners enlisted in the immediatist abolition cause—still a small mi-
nority of the Northern white population, but a noisy one that
agitated the slavery issue as never before in American history.

This pattern of sectional attack and counterattack would continue
over the ensuing decades, despite the best efforts of mainstream
politicians of both sections to eradicate it. Abolitionist activities led
to Southern efforts to shut off the flow of antislavery mailings from
the North and restrict discussion of slavery in Congress; Northern
repugnance at these abridgments of free expression strengthened
Northern opposition to slavery. In the 1840s, when the territorial
expansion that followed the Mexican War enlarged the sectional
controversies, the Northern antislavery cause began to turn into a
mass political movement, signaled by the rise in 1848 of the Free
Soil Party; Southern apprehension at these developments led to
increasingly determined defenses of slavery as a benevolent institution. Only twenty years after Walker published the first edition
of his *Appeal,* the once-marginal slavery question had become the
central issue in American politics. A dozen years later, white Americans would go to war against each other—and Walker's prophecy
would be fulfilled.

Or, more precisely, it would be partly fulfilled—for in the aftermath of the Civil War and emancipation, hopes for racial equality
were crushed. In this connection, Walker's *Appeal* retains its time-
liness. Even in freedom, succeeding generations of black Americans
had to endure the sorts of racism that Walker had seen everywhere
he journeyed in the 1820s. The legacies of that racism—not least
in black alienation and, for some, resignation—have continued to
accumulate over the decades. So, too, have the efforts to resist that
racism, with the development among African-Americans of a sin-
gular racial pride that is at once intensely American and also directly
at odds with complacent views of American freedom, equality, and
justice.

Walker's *Appeal* speaks with a particular eloquence to the continuing hurts, myths, and solidarities of race. The pamphlet has always had special significance for black readers. Its publication had an immediate and electrifying effect on younger black activists in the North. (Decades later, Frederick Douglass remembered the *Appeal* as one of the key abolitionist works, predating even Garrison's *Liberator*.) In 1848, the Troy, New York, black abolitionist Henry Highland Garnet reprinted the *Appeal* to coincide with the Free Soil campaign; since then, each generation of black activists and intellectuals has kept Walker's memory alive. And to read Walker's *Appeal* today is to encounter, with an eerie sense of contemporaneity, many of the issues and debates that have preoccupied black writers for the past century and a half.

Walker's remarks on education, and his defense of learning as a form of spiritual uplift, bring to mind the debates between Booker T. Washington and W.E.B. Du Bois that shook black Americans at the dawn of the twentieth century and that have not ended nearly a century later. Walker's caustic words about black submissiveness, his frightening apocalyptic passages, his vision of worldwide black unity, and his contempt for whites as his natural enemies all bring to mind the accents of the black nationalist politics that would emerge forcefully in the writings and speeches of Malcolm X. Similarly, his Christian beliefs, his hopeful vision of redemption, his practical alliances with whites, and his fundamental allegiances to a revolutionized version of American democratic ideals would find echoes in the exalted vision of Martin Luther King, Jr. Above all, Walker's portrayal of his divided self, at once a black and an American, foreshadowed what Du Bois would call the "double consciousness" of black America, a sense of doubleness that has formed a central theme—perhaps *the* central theme—of African-American art and letters.

Here then, with all of its mysteries, is a brief work of great importance. Abraham Lincoln spoke with some justice when he described Harriet Beecher Stowe as the lady who had written the book that caused the Civil War. But much of the controversy that preceded the publication of Stowe's *Uncle Tom's Cabin* can with almost equal justice be traced back to the publication of David Walker's *Appeal*. And in the *Appeal* there are presentments of the bitterness, defiance, and search for salvation that have marked

African-American history—and, thus, American history—ever since.

The text reprinted here is that of the third and final edition, as presented by Charles M. Wiltse in his 1965 edition of the *Appeal*. Except for corrections of some obvious typographical errors, Wiltse retained Walker's original spelling and punctuation. He also retained Walker's original footnotes and added some of his own, which he set off in brackets. I have silently altered a few of Wiltse's bracketed notes to accord with my introduction.

SEAN WILENTZ

Princeton, New Jersey
October 3, 1994

DAVID WALKER'S
APPEAL

☞ IT will be recollected, that I, in the first edition of my "Appeal," promised to demonstrate in the course of which, viz. in the course of my Appeal, to the satisfaction of the most incredulous mind, that we Coloured People of these United States, are, the most wretched, degraded and abject set of beings that ever lived since the world began, down to the present day, and, that, the white Christians of America, who hold us in slavery, (or, more properly speaking, pretenders to Christianity,) treat us more cruel and barbarous than any Heathen nation did any people whom it had subjected, or reduced to the same condition, that the Americans (who are, notwithstanding, looking for the Millennial day) have us. All I ask is, for a candid and careful perusal of this the third and last edition of my Appeal, where the world may see that we, the Blacks or Coloured People, are treated more cruel by the white Christians of America, than devils themselves ever treated a set of men, women and children on this earth.☜

☞ It is expected that all coloured men, women and children,* of every nation, language and tongue under heaven, will try to procure a copy of this Appeal and read it, or get some one to read it to them, for it is designed more particularly for them. Let them remember, that though our cruel oppressors and murderers, may (if possible) treat us more cruel, as Pharaoh did the children of Israel, yet the God of the Ethiopeans, has been pleased to hear our moans in consequence of oppression; and the day of our redemption from abject wretchedness draweth near, when we shall be enabled, in the most extended sense of the word, to stretch forth our hands to the LORD our GOD, but there must be a willingness on our part, for GOD to do these things for us, for we may be assured that he will not take us by the hairs of our head against our will and desire, and drag us from our very, mean, low and abject condition.☜

. * Who are not too deceitful, abject, and servile to resist the cruelties and murders inflicted upon us by the white slave holders, our enemies by nature.

PREAMBLE.

My dearly beloved Brethren and Fellow Citizens.

Having travelled over a considerable portion of these United States, and having, in the course of my travels, taken the most accurate observations of things as they exist—the result of my observations has warranted the full and unshaken conviction, that we, (coloured people of these United States,) are the most degraded, wretched, and abject set of beings that ever lived since the world began; and I pray God that none like us ever may live again until time shall be no more. They tell us of the Israelites in Egypt, the Helots in Sparta, and of the Roman Slaves, which last were made up from almost every nation under heaven, whose sufferings under those ancient and heathen nations, were, in comparison with ours, under this enlightened and Christian nation, no more than a cypher—or, in other words, those heathen nations of antiquity, had but little more among them than the name and form of slavery; while wretchedness and endless miseries were reserved, apparently in a phial, to be poured out upon our fathers, ourselves and our children, by *Christian* Americans!

These positions I shall endeavour, by the help of the Lord, to demonstrate in the course of this *Appeal*, to the satisfaction of the most incredulous mind—and may God Almighty, who is the Father of our Lord Jesus Christ, open your hearts to understand and believe the truth.

The *causes*, my brethren, which produce our wretchedness and miseries, are so very numerous and aggravating, that I believe the pen only of a Josephus or a Plutarch, can well enumerate and

explain them. Upon subjects, then, of such incomprehensible mag-
nitude, so impenetrable, and so notorious, I shall be obliged to
omit a large class of, and content myself with giving you an exposition of a few of those, which do indeed rage to such an alarm-
ing pitch, that they cannot but be a perpetual source of terror
and dismay to every reflecting mind.

I am fully aware, in making this appeal to my much afflicted
and suffering brethren, that I shall not only be assailed by those
whose greatest earthly desires are, to keep us in abject ignorance
and wretchedness, and who are of the firm conviction that Heaven
has designed us and our children to be slaves and *beasts of burden* to them and their children. I say, I do not only expect to be
held up to the public as an ignorant, impudent and restless dis-
turber of the public peace, by such avaricious creatures, as well
as a mover of insubordination—and perhaps put in prison or to
death, for giving a superficial exposition of our miseries, and ex-
posing tyrants. But I am persuaded, that many of my brethren,
particularly those who are ignorantly in league with slave-holders
or tyrants, who acquire their daily bread by the blood and sweat
of their more ignorant brethren—and not a few of those too,
who are too ignorant to see an inch beyond their noses, will rise
up and call me cursed—Yea, the jealous ones among us will perhaps use more abject subtlety, by affirming that this work is not
worth perusing, that we are well situated, and there is no use in
trying to better our condition, for we cannot. I will ask one question here.—Can our condition be any worse?—Can it be more
mean and abject? If there are any changes, will they not be for
the better, though they may appear for the worst at first? Can
they get us any lower? Where can they get us? They are afraid
to treat us worse, for they know well, the day they do it they are
gone. But against all accusations which may or can be preferred
against me, I appeal to Heaven for my motive in writing—who
knows that my object is, if possible, to awaken in the breasts of
my afflicted, degraded and slumbering brethren, a spirit of inquiry and investigation respecting our miseries and wretchedness
in this *Republican Land of Liberty! ! ! ! ! !*

The sources from which our miseries are derived, and on which
I shall comment, I shall not combine in one, but shall put them
under distinct heads and expose them in their turn; in doing

which, keeping truth on my side, and not departing from the strictest rules of morality, I shall endeavour to penetrate, search out, and lay them open for your inspection. If you cannot or will not profit by them, I shall have done *my* duty to you, my country and my God.

And as the inhuman system of *slavery*, is the *source* from which most of our miseries proceed, I shall begin with that *curse to nations*, which has spread terror and devastation through so many nations of antiquity, and which is raging to such a pitch at the present day in Spain and in Portugal. It had one tug in England, in France, and in the United States of America; yet the inhabitants thereof, do not learn wisdom, and erase it entirely from their dwellings and from all with whom they have to do. The fact is, the labour of slaves comes so cheap to the avaricious usurpers, and is (as they think) of such great utility to the country where it exists, that those who are actuated by sordid avarice only, overlook the evils, which will as sure as the Lord lives, follow after the good. In fact, they are so happy to keep in ignorance and degradation, and to receive the homage and the labour of the slaves, they forget that God rules in the armies of heaven and among the inhabitants of the earth, having his ears continually open to the cries, tears and groans of his oppressed people; and being a just and holy Being will at one day appear fully in behalf of the oppressed, and arrest the progress of the avaricious oppressors; for although the destruction of the oppressors God may not effect by the oppressed, yet the Lord our God will bring other destructions upon them—for not unfrequently will he cause them to rise up one against another, to be split and divided, and to oppress each other, and sometimes to open hostilities with sword in hand. Some may ask, what is the matter with this united and happy people?—Some say it is the cause of political usurpers, tyrants, oppressors, &c. But has not the Lord an oppressed and suffering people among them? Does the Lord condescend to hear their cries and see their tears in consequence of oppression? Will he let the oppressors rest comfortably and happy always? Will he not cause the very children of the oppressors to rise up against them, and oftimes put them to death? "God works in many ways his wonders to perform."

I will not here speak of the destructions which the Lord

brought upon Egypt, in consequence of the oppression and consequent groans of the oppressed—of the hundreds and thousands of Egyptians whom God hurled into the Red Sea for afflicting his people in their land—of the Lord's suffering people in Sparta or Lacedaemon, the land of the truly famous Lycurgus—nor have I time to comment upon the cause which produced the fierceness with which Sylla usurped the title, and absolutely acted as dictator of the Roman people—the conspiracy of Cataline—the conspiracy against, and murder of Cæsar in the Senate house—the spirit with which Marc Antony made himself master of the commonwealth—his associating Octavius and Lipidus with himself in power—their dividing the provinces of Rome among themselves—their attack and defeat, on the plains of Phillippi, of the last defenders of their liberty, (Brutus and Cassius)—the tyranny of Tiberius, and from him to the final overthrow of Constantinople by the Turkish Sultan, Mahomed II. A. D. 1453. I say, I shall not take up time to speak of the *causes* which produced so much wretchedness and massacre among those heathen nations, for I am aware that you know too well, that God is just, as well as merciful!—I shall call your attention a few moments to that *Christian* nation, the Spaniards—while I shall leave almost unnoticed, that avaricious and cruel people, the Portuguese, among whom all true hearted Christians and lovers of Jesus Christ, must evidently see the judgments of God displayed. To show the judgments of God upon the Spaniards, I shall occupy but a little time, leaving a plenty of room for the candid and unprejudiced to reflect.

All persons who are acquainted with history, and particularly the Bible, who are not blinded by the God of this world, and are not actuated solely by avarice—who are able to lay aside prejudice long enough to view candidly and impartially, things as they were, are, and probably will be—who are willing to admit that God made man to serve Him *alone,* and that man should have no other Lord or Lords but Himself—that God Almighty is the *sole proprietor* or *master* of the WHOLE human family, and will not on any consideration admit of a colleague, being unwilling to divide his glory with another—and who can dispense with prejudice long enough to admit that we are *men*, notwithstanding our *improminent noses* and *woolly heads,* and believe that we feel for our fathers, mothers, wives and children, as well as the whites do for theirs.—I say, all who are permitted to see and believe these things, can easily recognize the judgments of God among the Spaniards. Though others may lay the cause of the fierceness with which they cut each other's throats, to some other circumstance, yet they who believe that God is a God of justice, will believe that SLAVERY *is the principal cause.*

While the Spaniards are running about upon the field of battle cutting each other's throats, has not the Lord an afflicted and suffering people in the midst of them, whose cries and groans in consequence of oppression are continually pouring into the ears of the God of justice? Would they not cease to cut each other's throats, if they could? But how can they? The very support which they draw from government to aid them in perpetrating such enormities, does it not arise in a great degree from the wretched victims of oppression among them? And yet they are calling for *Peace!—Peace! !* Will any peace be given unto them? Their destruction may indeed be procrastinated awhile, but can it continue long, while they are oppressing the Lord's people? Has He not the hearts of all men in His hand? Will he suffer one part of his creatures to go on oppressing another like brutes always, with impunity? And yet, those avaricious wretches are calling for *Peace! ! ! !* I declare, it does appear to me, as though some nations think God is asleep, or that he made the Africans for nothing else but to dig their mines and work their farms, or they cannot believe history, sacred or profane. I ask every man who has a heart, and is blessed with the privilege of believing—Is not God a God of justice to *all* his creatures? Do you say he is? Then if he gives peace and tranquillity to tyrants, and permits them to keep our fathers, our mothers, ourselves and our children in eternal ignorance and wretchedness, to support them and their families, would he be to us a God of *justice?* I ask, O ye *Christians! ! !* who hold us and our children in the most abject ignorance and degradation, that ever a people were afflicted with since the world began—I say, if God gives you peace and tranquillity, and suffers you thus to go on afflicting us, and our children, who have never given you the least provocation— would he be to us *a God of justice?* If you will allow that we are MEN, who feel for each other, does not the blood of our fathers and of us their children, cry aloud to the Lord of Sabaoth against you, for the cruelties and murders with which you have, and do continue to afflict us. But it is time for me to close my remarks on the suburbs, just to enter more fully into the interior of this system of cruelty and oppression.

ARTICLE I.

My beloved brethren:—The Indians of North and of South America—the Greeks—the Irish, subjected under the king of Great Britain—the Jews, that ancient people of the Lord—the inhabitants of the islands of the sea—in fine, all the inhabitants of the earth, (except however, the sons of Africa) are called *men,* and of course are, and ought to be free. But we, (coloured people) and our children are *brutes! !* and of course are, and *ought to be* SLAVES to the American people and their children forever! ! to dig their mines and work their farms; and thus go on enriching them, from one generation to another with our *blood* and our *tears! ! ! !*

I promised in a preceding page to demonstrate to the satisfaction of the most incredulous, that we, (coloured people of these United States of America) are the *most wretched, degraded* and *abject* set of beings that *ever lived* since the world began, and that the white Americans having reduced us to the wretched state of *slavery,* treat us in that condition *more cruel* (they being an enlightened and Christian people,) than any heathen nation did any people whom it had reduced to our condition. These affirmations are so well confirmed in the minds of all unprejudiced men, who have taken the trouble to read histories, that they need no elucidation from me. But to put them beyond all doubt, I refer you in the first place to the children of Jacob, or of Israel in Egypt,

7

under Pharaoh and his people. Some of my brethren do not know who Pharaoh and the Egyptians were—I know it to be a fact, that some of them take the Egyptians to have been a gang of *devils,* not knowing any better, and that they (Egyptians) having got possession of the Lord's people, treated them *nearly* as cruel as *Christian Americans* do us, at the present day. For the information of such, I would only mention that the Egyptians, were Africans or coloured people, such as we are—some of them yellow and others dark—a mixture of Ethiopians and the natives of Egypt—about the same as you see the coloured people of the United States at the present day.—I say, I call your attention then, to the children of Jacob, while I point out particularly to you his son Joseph, among the rest, in Egypt.

"And Pharaoh, said unto Joseph, . . . thou shalt be over my house, and according unto thy word shall all my people be ruled: only in the throne will I be greater than thou.*

"And Pharaoh said unto Joseph, see, I have set thee over all the land of Egypt." †

"And Pharaoh said unto Joseph, I am Pharaoh, and without thee shall no man lift up his hand or foot in all the land of Egypt." ‡

Now I appeal to heaven and to earth, and particularly to the American people themselves, who cease not to declare that our condition is not *hard,* and that we are comparatively satisfied to rest in wretchedness and misery, under them and their children. Not, indeed, to show me a coloured President, a Governor, a Legislator, a Senator, a Mayor, or an Attorney at the Bar.—But to show me a man of colour, who holds the low office of a Constable, or one who sits in a Juror Box, even on a case of one of his wretched brethren, throughout this great Republic! !—But let us pass Joseph the son of Israel a little farther in review, as he existed with that heathen nation.

"And Pharaoh called Joseph's name Zaphnathpaaneah; and he gave him to wife Asenath the daughter of Potipherah priest of On. And Joseph went out over all the land of Egypt." §

---

* See Genesis, chap. xli. [39-40].
† [xli. 41.]
[‡] xli. 44.
§ xli. 45.

Compare the above, with the American institutions. Do they not institute laws to prohibit us from marrying among the whites? I would wish, candidly, however, before the Lord, to be understood, that I would not give a *pinch of snuff* to be married to any white person I ever saw in all the days of my life. And I do say it, that the black man, or man of colour, who will leave his own colour (provided he can get one, who is good for any thing) and marry a white woman, to be a double slave to her, just because she is *white*, ought to be treated by her as he surely will be, viz: as a NIGGER! ! ! ! It is not, indeed, what I care about inter-marriages with the whites, which induced me to pass this subject in review; for the Lord knows, that there is a day coming when they will be glad enough to get into the company of the blacks, notwithstanding, we are, in this generation, levelled by them, almost on a level with the brute creation: and some of us they treat even worse than they do the brutes that perish. I only made this extract to show how much lower we are held, and how much more cruel we are treated by the Americans, than were the children of Jacob, by the Egyptians.—We will notice the sufferings of Israel some further, under *heathen Pharaoh,* compared with ours under the *enlightened Christians of America.*

"And Pharaoh spoke unto Joseph, saying, thy father and thy brethren are come unto thee:

"The land of Egypt is before thee: in the best of the land make thy father and brethren to dwell; in the land of Goshen let them dwell: and if thou knowest any men of activity among them, then make them rulers over my cattle." *

I ask those people who treat us so *well*, Oh! I ask them, where is the most barren spot of land which they have given unto us? Israel had the most fertile land in all Egypt. Need I mention the very notorious fact, that I have known a poor man of colour, who laboured night and day, to acquire a little money, and having acquired it, he vested it in a small piece of land, and got him a house erected thereon, and having paid for the whole, he moved his family into it, where he was suffered to remain but nine months, when he was cheated out of his property by a white man,

* Genesis, chap. xlvii. 5, 6.

and driven out of door! And is not this the case generally? Can
a man of colour buy a piece of land and keep it peaceably? Will
not some white man try to get it from him, even if it is in a *mud
hole?* I need not comment any farther on a subject, which all,
both black and white, will readily admit. But I must, really, observe that in this very city, when a man of colour dies, if he
owned any real estate it most generally falls into the hands of
some white person. The wife and children of the deceased may
weep and lament if they please, but the estate will be kept snug
enough by its white possessor.

But to prove farther that the condition of the Israelites was
better under the Egyptians than ours is under the whites. I call
upon the professing Christians, I call upon the philanthropist, I
call upon the very tyrant himself, to show me a page of history,
either sacred or profane, on which a verse can be found, which
maintains, that the Egyptians heaped the *insupportable insult*
upon the children of Israel, by telling them that they were not
of the *human family.* Can the whites deny this charge? Have
they not, after having reduced us to the deplorable condition of
slaves under their feet, held us up as descending originally from
the tribes of *Monkeys* or *Orang-Outangs?* O! my God! I appeal
to every man of feeling—is not this insupportable? Is it not
heaping the most gross insult upon our miseries, because they
have got us under their feet and we cannot help ourselves? Oh!
pity us we pray thee, Lord Jesus, Master.—Has Mr. Jefferson
declared to the world, that we are inferior to the whites, both in
the endowments of our bodies and our minds? * It is indeed surprising, that a man of such great learning, combined with such
excellent natural parts, should speak so of a set of men in chains.
I do not know what to compare it to, unless, like putting one wild
deer in an iron cage, where it will be secured, and hold another
by the side of the same, then let it go, and expect the one in the
cage to run as fast as the one at liberty. So far, my brethren,
were the Egyptians from heaping these insults upon their slaves,
that Pharaoh's daughter took Moses, a son of Israel for her own,
as will appear by the following.

"And Pharaoh's daughter said unto her, [Moses' mother] take

---

* [The reference is to Jefferson's *Notes on Virginia,* Query XIV. All of Walker's references to Jefferson are to this section of the *Notes.* Ed.]

this child away, and nurse it for me, and I will pay thee thy wages. And the woman took the child [Moses] and nursed it.

"And the child grew, and she brought him unto Pharaoh's daughter and he became her son. And she called his name Moses: and she said because I drew him out of the water." *

In all probability, Moses would have become Prince Regent to the throne, and no doubt, in process of time but he would have been seated on the throne of Egypt. But he had rather suffer shame, with the people of God, than to enjoy pleasures with that wicked people for a season. O! that the coloured people were long since of Moses' excellent disposition, instead of courting favour with, and telling news and lies to our *natural enemies,* against each other—aiding them to keep their hellish chains of slavery upon us. Would we not long before this time, have been respectable men, instead of such wretched victims of oppression as we are? Would they be able to drag our mothers, our fathers, our wives, our children and ourselves, around the world in chains and hand-cuffs as they do, to dig up gold and silver for them and theirs? This question, my brethren, I leave for you to digest; and may God Almighty force it home to your hearts. Remember that unless you are united, keeping your tongues within your teeth, you will be afraid to trust your secrets to each other, and thus perpetuate our miseries under the *Christians! ! ! !* ☞ ADDITION.—Remember, also to lay humble at the feet of our Lord and Master Jesus Christ, with prayers and fastings. Let our enemies go on with their butcheries, and at once fill up their cup. Never make an attempt to gain our freedom or *natural right,* from under our cruel oppressors and murderers, until you see your way clear†—when that hour arrives and you move, be not

* See Exodus, chap. ii. 9, 10.

† It is not to be understood here, that I mean for us to wait until God shall take us by the hair of our heads and drag us out of abject wretchedness and slavery, nor do I mean to convey the idea for us to wait until our enemies shall make preparations, and call us to seize those preparations, take it away from them, and put every thing before us to death, in order to gain our freedom which God has given us. For you must remember that we are men as well as they. God has been pleased to give us two eyes, two hands, two feet, and some sense in our heads as well as they. They have no more right to hold us in slavery than we have to hold them, we have just as much right, in the sight of God, to hold them and their children in slavery and wretchedness, as they have to hold us, and no more.

afraid or dismayed; for be you assured that Jesus Christ the King of heaven and of earth who is the God of justice and of armies, will surely go before you. And those enemies who have for hundreds of years stolen our *rights*, and kept us ignorant of Him and His divine worship, he will remove. Millions of whom, are this day, so ignorant and avaricious, that they cannot conceive how God can have an attribute of justice, and show mercy to us because it pleased Him to make us black—which colour, Mr. Jefferson calls unfortunate! ! ! ! ! ! As though we are not as thankful to our God, for having made us as it pleased himself, as they, (the whites,) are for having made them white. They think because they hold us in their infernal chains of slavery, that we wish to be white, or of their color—but they are dreadfully deceived—we wish to be just as it pleased our Creator to have made us, and no avaricious and unmerciful wretches, have any business to make slaves of, or hold us in slavery. How would they like for us to make slaves of, and hold them in cruel slavery, and murder them as they do us?—But is Mr. Jefferson's assertions true? viz. "that it is unfortunate for us that our Creator has been pleased to make us *black*." We will not take his say so, for the fact. The world will have an opportunity to see whether it is unfortunate for us, that our Creator *has made us* darker than the *whites*.

Fear not the number and education of our *enemies*, against whom we shall have to contend for our lawful right; guaranteed to us by our Maker; for why should we be afraid, when God is, and will continue, (if we continue humble) to be on our side?

The man who would not fight under our Lord and Master Jesus Christ, in the glorious and heavenly cause of freedom and of God—to be delivered from the most wretched, abject and servile slavery, that ever a people was afflicted with since the foundation of the world, to the present day—ought to be kept with all of his children or family, in slavery, or in chains, to be butchered by his *cruel enemies.*

I saw a paragraph, a few years since, in a South Carolina paper, which, speaking of the barbarity of the Turks, it said: "The Turks are the most barbarous people in the world—they treat the Greeks more like *brutes* than human beings." And in the same paper was an advertisement, which said: "Eight well built Virginia and Maryland *Negro fellows* and four *wenches* will positively be *sold* this day, *to the highest bidder!*" And what astonished me still more was, to see in this same. *humane* paper! ! the cuts of three men, with clubs and budgets on their backs, and an advertisement offering a considerable sum of money for their apprehension and delivery. I declare, it is really so amusing to hear the Southerners and Westerners of this country talk about *barbarity*, that it is positively, enough to make a man *smile*.

The sufferings of the Helots among the Spartans, were somewhat severe, it is true, but to say that theirs, were as severe as ours among the Americans, I do most strenuously deny—for instance, can any man show me an article on a page of ancient history which specifies, that, the Spartans chained, and handcuffed the Helots, and dragged them from their wives and children, children from their parents, mothers from their suckling babes, wives from their husbands, driving them from one end of the country to the other? Notice the Spartans were heathens, who lived long before our Divine Master made his appearance in the flesh. Can Christian Americans deny these barbarous cruelties? Have you not, Americans, having subjected us under you, added to these miseries, by insulting us in telling us to our face, because we are helpless, that we are not of the human family? I ask you, O! Americans, I ask you, in the name of the Lord, can you deny these charges? Some perhaps may deny, by saying, that they never thought or said that we were not men. But do not actions speak louder than words?—have they not made provisions for the Greeks, and Irish? Nations who have never done the least thing for them, while *we*, who have enriched their country with our blood and tears—have dug up gold and silver for them and their children, from generation to generation, and are in more miseries than any other people under heaven, are not seen, but by comparatively, a handful of the American people? There are indeed, more ways to kill a dog, besides choking it to death with butter. Further—The Spartans or Lacedaemonians, had some frivolous pretext, for enslaving the Helots, for they (Helots) while being free inhabitants of Sparta, stirred up an intestine commotion, and were, by the Spartans subdued, and made prisoners of war. Consequently they and their children were condemned to perpetual slavery.*

I have been for years troubling the pages of historians, to find out what our fathers have done to the *white Christians of America*, to merit such condign punishment as they have inflicted on them, and do continue to inflict on us their children. But I must aver, that my researches have hitherto been to no effect. I have therefore, come to the immoveable conclusion, that they (Americans) have, and do continue to punish us for nothing else, but for enriching them and their country. For I cannot conceive of anything else. Nor will I ever believe otherwise, until the Lord shall convince me.

The world knows, that slavery as it existed among the Romans, (which was the primary cause of their destruction) was, comparatively speaking, no more than a *cypher*, when compared with ours under the Americans. Indeed I should not have noticed the Roman slaves, had not the very learned and penetrating Mr. Jefferson said, "when a master was murdered, all his slaves in the same house, or within hearing, were condemned to death." †
—Here let me ask Mr. Jefferson, (but he is gone to answer at the bar of God, for the deeds done in his body while living,) I therefore ask the whole American people, had I not rather die, or be put to death, than to be a slave to any tyrant, who takes not only my own, but my wife and children's lives by the inches? Yea, would I meet death with avidity far! far! ! in preference to such *servile submission* to the murderous hands of tyrants. Mr. Jefferson's very severe remarks on us have been so extensively argued upon by men whose attainments in literature, I shall never be able to reach, that I would not have meddled with it, were it not to solicit each of my brethren, who has the spirit of a man, to buy a copy of Mr. Jefferson's "Notes on Virginia," and put it in the hand of his son. For let no one of us suppose that the refutations which have been written by our white friends are

---

* See Dr. Goldsmith's History of Greece—page 9. See also, Plutarch's Lives. The Helots subdued by Agis, king of *Sparta*. [Walker's citation is to Oliver Goldsmith, *A History of Greece from the Earliest State to the Death of Alexander the Great*. Fifth American edition, 2 vols. in 1, Philadelphia, 1817. Ed.]
† See his Notes on Virginia, page 210.

enough—they are *whites*—we are *blacks*. We, and the world wish to see the charges of Mr. Jefferson refuted by the blacks *themselves*, according to their chance; for we must remember that what the whites have written respecting this subject, is other men's labours, and did not emanate from the blacks. I know well, that there are some talents and learning among the coloured people of this country, which we have not a chance to develope, in consequence of oppression; but our oppression ought not to hinder us from acquiring all we can. For we will have a chance to develope them by and by. God will not suffer us, always to be oppressed. Our sufferings will come to an *end*, in spite of all the Americans this side of *eternity*. Then we will want all the learning and talents among ourselves, and perhaps more, to govern ourselves.—"Every dog must have its day," the American's is coming to an end.

But let us review Mr. Jefferson's remarks respecting us some further. Comparing our miserable fathers, with the learned philosophers of Greece, he says: "Yet notwithstanding these and other discouraging circumstances among the Romans, their slaves were often their rarest artists. They excelled too, in science, insomuch as to be usually employed as tutors to their master's children; Epictetus, Terence and Phædrus, were slaves,—but they were of the race of whites. It is not their *condition* then, but *nature*, which has produced the distinction."* See this, my brethren! ! Do you believe that this assertion is swallowed by millions of the whites? Do you know that Mr. Jefferson was one of as great characters as ever lived among the whites? See his writings for the world, and public labours for the United States of America. Do you believe that the assertions of such a man, will pass away into oblivion unobserved by this people and the world? If you do you are much mistaken—See how the American people treat us—have we souls in our bodies? Are we men who have any spirits at all? I know that there are many *swellbellied* fellows among us, whose greatest object is to fill their stomachs. Such I do not mean—I am after those who know and feel, that we are MEN, as well as other people; to them, I say, that unless we try to refute Mr. Jefferson's arguments respecting us, we will only establish them.

* See his Notes on Virginia, page 211.

But the slaves among the Romans. Every body who has read history, knows, that as soon as a slave among the Romans obtained his freedom, he could rise to the greatest eminence in the State, and there was no law instituted to hinder a slave from buying his freedom. Have not the Americans instituted laws to hinder us from obtaining our freedom? Do any deny this charge? Read the laws of Virginia, North Carolina, &c. Further: have not the Americans instituted laws to prohibit a man of colour from obtaining and holding any office whatever, under the government of the United States of America? Now, Mr. Jefferson tells us, that our condition is not so hard, as the slaves were under the Romans! ! ! ! ! !

It is time for me to bring this article to a close. But before I close it, I must observe to my brethren that at the close of the first Revolution in this country, with Great Britain, there were but thirteen States in the Union, now there are twenty-four, most of which are slave-holding States, and the whites are dragging us around in chains and in handcuffs, to their new States and Territories to work their mines and farms, to enrich them and their children—and millions of them believing firmly that we being a little darker than they, were made by our Creator to be an inheritance to them and their children for ever—the same as a parcel of *brutes*.

Are we MEN! !—I ask you, O my brethren! are we MEN? Did our Creator make us to be slaves to dust and ashes like ourselves? Are they not dying worms as well as we? Have they not to make their appearance before the tribunal of Heaven, to answer for the deeds done in the body, as well as we? Have we any other Master but Jesus Christ alone? Is he not their Master as well as ours?—What right then, have we to obey and call any other Master, but Himself? How we could be so *submissive* to a gang of men, whom we cannot tell whether they are *as good* as ourselves or not, I never could conceive. However, this is shut up with the Lord, and we cannot precisely tell—but I declare, we judge men by their works.

The whites have always been an unjust, jealous, unmerciful, avaricious and blood-thirsty set of beings, always seeking after power and authority.—We view them all over the confederacy of

Greece, where they were first known to be any thing, (in consequence of education) we see them there, cutting each other's
throats—trying to subject each other to wretchedness and misery
—to effect which, they used all kinds of deceitful, unfair, and
unmerciful means. We view them next in Rome, where the
spirit of tyranny and deceit raged still higher. We view them in
Gaul, Spain, and in Britain.—In fine, we view them all over
Europe, together with what were scattered about in Asia and
Africa, as heathens, and we see them acting more like devils
than accountable men. But some may ask, did not the blacks
of Africa, and the mulattoes of Asia, go on in the same way
as did the whites of Europe. I answer, no—they never were
half so avaricious, deceitful and unmerciful as the whites, according to their knowledge.

But we will leave the whites or Europeans as heathens, and
take a view of them as Christians, in which capacity we see them
as cruel, if not more so than ever. In fact, take them as a body,
they are ten times more cruel, avaricious and unmerciful than
ever they were; for while they were heathens, they were bad
enough it is true, but it is positively a fact that they were not
quite so audacious as to go and take vessel loads of men, women
and children, and in cold blood, and through devilishness, throw
them into the sea, and murder them in all kind of ways. While
they were heathens, they were too ignorant for such barbarity.
But being Christians, enlightened and sensible, they are completely prepared for such hellish cruelties. Now suppose God
were to give them more sense, what would they do? If it were
possible, would they not *dethrone* Jehovah and seat themselves
upon his throne? I therefore, in the name and fear of the Lord
God of Heaven and of earth, divested of prejudice either on the
side of my colour or that of the whites, advance my suspicion
of them, whether they are *as good by nature* as we are or not.
Their actions, since they were known as a people, have been the
reverse, I do indeed suspect them, but this, as I before observed,
is shut up with the Lord, we cannot exactly tell, it will be proved
in succeeding generations.—The whites have had the essence of
the gospel as it was preached by my master and his apostles—
the Ethiopians have not, who are to have it in its meridian

splendor—the Lord will give it to them to their satisfaction. I hope and pray my God, that they will make good use of it, that it may be well with them.*

* It is my solemn belief, that if ever the world becomes Christianized, (which must certainly take place before long) it will be through the means, under God of the *Blacks,* who are now held in wretchedness, and degradation, by the white *Christians* of the world, who before they learn to do justice to us before our Maker—and be reconciled to us, and reconcile us to them, and by that means have clear consciences before God and man.—Send out Missionaries to convert the Heathens, many of whom after they cease to worship gods, which neither see nor hear, become ten times more the children of Hell, then ever they were, why what is the reason? Why the reason is obvious, they must learn to do justice at home, before they go into distant lands, to display their charity, Christianity, and benevolence; when they learn to do justice, God will accept their offering, (no man may think that I am against Missionaries for I am not, my object is to see justice done at home, before we go to convert the Heathens.)

ARTICLE II.

Ignorance, my brethren, is a mist, low down into the very dark and almost impenetrable abyss in which, our fathers for many centuries have been plunged. The Christians, and enlightened of Europe, and some of Asia, seeing the ignorance and consequent degradation of our fathers, instead of trying to enlighten them, by teaching them that religion and light with which God had blessed them, they have plunged them into wretchedness ten thousand times more intolerable, than if they had left them entirely to the Lord, and to add to their miseries, deep down into which they have plunged them tell them, that they are an *inferior* and *distinct race* of beings, which they will be glad enough to recall and swallow by and by. Fortune and misfortune, two inseparable companions, lay rolled up in the wheel of events, which have from the creation of the world, and will continue to take place among men until God shall dash worlds together.

When we take a retrospective view of the arts and sciences—the wise legislators—the Pyramids, and other magnificent buildings—the turning of the channel of the river Nile, by the sons of Africa or of Ham, among whom learning originated, and was carried thence into Greece, where it was improved upon and refined. Thence among the Romans, and all over the then enlightened parts of the world, and it has been enlightening the dark and benighted minds of men from then, down to this day. I say, when I view retrospectively, the renown of that once mighty

people, the children of our great progenitor I am indeed cheered.
Yea further, when I view that mighty son of Africa, HANNIBAL,
one of the greatest generals of antiquity, who defeated and cut
off so many thousands of the white Romans or murderers, and
who carried his victorious arms, to the very gate of Rome, and
I give it as my candid opinion, that had Carthage been well
united and had given him good support, he would have carried
that cruel and barbarous city by storm. But they were dis-united,
as the coloured people are now, in the United States of America,
the reason our natural enemies are enabled to keep their feet on
our throats.

Beloved brethren—here let me tell you, and believe it, that
the Lord our God, as true as he sits on his throne in heaven, and
as true as our Saviour died to redeem the world, will give you
a Hannibal, and when the Lord shall have raised him up, and
given him to you for your possession, O my suffering brethren!
remember the divisions and consequent sufferings of *Carthage*
and of *Hayti*. Read the history particularly of Hayti, and see
how they were butchered by the whites, and do you take warning.
The person whom God shall give you, give him your support
and let him go his length, and behold in him the salvation of
your God. God will indeed, deliver you through him from your
deplorable and wretched condition under the Christians of
America. I charge you this day before my God to lay no obstacle in his way, but let him go.

The whites want slaves, and want us for their slaves, but some
of them will curse the day they ever saw us. As true as the sun
ever shone in its meridian splendor, my colour will root some of
them out of the very face of the earth. They shall have enough
of making slaves of, and butchering, and murdering us in the
manner which they have. No doubt some may say that I write
with a bad spirit, and that I being a black, wish these things to
occur. Whether I write with a bad or a good spirit, I say if these
things do not occur in their proper time, it is because the world
in which we live does not exist, and we are deceived with regard
to its existence.—It is immaterial however to me, who believe, or
who refuse—though I should like to see the whites repent perad-
venture God may have mercy on them, some however, have gone
so far that their cup must be filled.

But what need have I to refer to antiquity, when Hayti, the glory of the blacks and terror of tyrants, is enough to convince the most avaricious and stupid of wretches—which is at this time, and I am sorry to say it, plagued with that scourge of nations, the Catholic religion; but I hope and pray God that she may yet rid herself of it, and adopt in its stead the Protestant faith; also, I hope that she may keep peace within her borders and be united, keeping a strict look out for tyrants, for if they get the least chance to injure her, they will avail themselves of it, as true as the Lord lives in heaven. But one thing which gives me joy is, that they are men who would be cut off to a man, before they would yield to the combined forces of the whole world—in fact, if the whole world was combined against them, it could not do any thing with them, unless the Lord delivers them up.

Ignorance and treachery one against the other—a grovelling servile and abject submission to the lash of tyrants, we see plainly, my brethren, are not the natural elements of the blacks, as the Americans try to make us believe; but these are misfortunes which God has suffered our fathers to be enveloped in for many ages, no doubt in consequence of their disobedience to their Maker, and which do, indeed, reign at this time among us, almost to the destruction of all other principles: for I must truly say, that ignorance, the mother of treachery and deceit, gnaws into our very vitals. Ignorance, as it now exists among us, produces a state of things, Oh my Lord! too horrible to present to the world. Any man who is curious to see the full force of ignorance developed among the coloured people of the United States of America, has only to go into the southern and western states of this confederacy, where, if he is not a tyrant, but has the feelings of a human being, who can feel for a fellow creature, he may see enough to make his very heart bleed! He may see there, a son take his mother, who bore almost the pains of death to give him birth, and by the command of a tyrant, strip her as naked as she came into the world, and apply the cow-hide to her, until she falls a victim to death in the road! He may see a husband take his dear wife, not unfrequently in a pregnant state, and perhaps far advanced, and beat her for an unmerciful wretch, until his infant falls a lifeless lump at her feet! Can the Americans escape God Almighty? If they do, can he be to us

a God of Justice? God is just, and I know it—for he has con-
vinced me to my satisfaction—I cannot doubt him. My observer
may see fathers beating their sons, mothers their daughters, and
children their parents, all to pacify the passions of unrelenting
tyrants. He may also, see them telling news and lies, making
mischief one upon another. These are some of the productions
of ignorance, which he will see practised among my dear brethren,
who are held in unjust slavery and wretchedness, by avaricious
and unmerciful tyrants, to whom, and their hellish deeds, I
would suffer my life to be taken before I would submit. And
when my curious observer comes to take notice of those who are
said to be free, (which assertion I deny) and who are making
some frivolous pretentions to common sense, he will see that
branch of ignorance among the slaves assuming a more cunning
and deceitful course of procedure.—He may see some of my
brethren in league with tyrants, selling their own brethren into
hell upon earth, not dissimilar to the exhibitions in Africa, but
in a more secret, servile and abject manner. Oh Heaven! I am
full! ! ! I can hardly move my pen! ! ! ! and as I expect some
will try to put me to death, to strike terror into others, and to
obliterate from their minds the notion of freedom, so as to keep
my brethren the more secure in wretchedness, where they will be
permitted to stay but a short time (whether tyrants believe it or
not)—I shall give the world a development of facts, which are
already witnessed in the courts of heaven. My observer may see
some of those ignorant and treacherous creatures (coloured
people) sneaking about in the large cities, endeavouring to find
out all strange coloured people, where they work and where they
reside, asking them questions, and trying to ascertain whether
they are runaways or not, telling them, at the same time, that
they always have been, are, and always will be, friends to their
brethren; and, perhaps, that they themselves are absconders,
and a thousand such treacherous lies to get the better information
of the more ignorant! ! ! There have been and are at this day
in Boston, New-York, Philadelphia, and Baltimore, coloured men,
who are in league with tyrants, and who receive a great portion
of their daily bread, of the moneys which they acquire from the
blood and tears of their more miserable brethren, whom they

scandalously delivered into the hands of our *natural ene-mies! ! ! ! ! !*

To show the force of degraded ignorance and deceit among us some farther, I will give here an extract from a paragraph, which may be found in the Columbian Centinel of this city, for September 9, 1829, on the first page of which, the curious may find an article, headed ·

"AFFRAY AND MURDER."
"Portsmouth, (Ohio) Aug. 22, 1829.

"A most shocking outrage was committed in Kentucky, about eight miles from this place, on 14th inst. A negro driver, by the name of Gordon, who had purchased in Maryland about sixty negroes, was taking them, assisted by an associate named Allen, and the wagoner who conveyed the baggage, to the Mississippi. The men were hand-cuffed and chained together, in the usual manner for driving those poor wretches, while the women and children were suffered to proceed without incumbrance. It appears that, by means of a file the negroes, unobserved, had succeeded in separating the iron which bound their hands, in such a way as to be able to throw them off at any moment. About 8 o'clock in the morning, while proceeding on the state road leading from Greenup to Vanceburg, two of them dropped their shackles and commenced a fight, when the wagoner (Petit) rushed in with his whip to compel them to desist. At this moment, every negro was found to be perfectly at liberty; and one of them seizing a club, gave Petit a violent blow on the head, and laid him dead at his feet; and Allen, who came to his assistance, met a similar fate, from the contents of a pistol fired by another of the gang. Gordon was then attacked, seized and held by one of the negroes, whilst another fired twice at him with a pistol, the ball of which each time grazed his head, but not proving effectual, he was beaten with clubs, and left for dead. They then commenced pillaging the wagon, and with an axe split open the trunk of Gordon, and rifled it of the money, about $2,400. Sixteen of the negroes then took to the woods; Gordon, in the mean time, not being materially injured, was enabled, by the assistance of one of the women, to mount his horse and flee; pursued, however, by one of the gang on another horse, with a drawn pistol; fortunately he escaped with his life barely, arriving at a plantation, as the negro came in sight; who then turned about and retreated.

"The neighbourhood was immediately rallied, and a hot pursuit given—which, we understand, has resulted in the capture of the whole gang and the recovery of the greatest part of the money. Seven of the negro men and one woman, it is said were engaged in the murders, and will be brought to trial at the next court in Greenupsburg."

Here my brethren, I want you to notice particularly in the above article, the *ignorant* and *deceitful actions* of this coloured woman. I beg you to view it candidly, as for ETERNITY! ! ! ! Here a *notorious wretch,* with two other confederates had SIXTY of them in a gang, driving them like *brutes*—the men all in chains and hand-cuffs, and by the help of God they got their chains and hand-cuffs thrown off, and caught two of the wretches and put them to death, and beat the other until they thought he was dead, and left him for dead; however, he deceived them, and rising from the ground, this *servile woman* helped him upon his horse, and he made his escape. Brethren, what do you think of this? Was it the natural *fine feelings* of this woman, to save such a wretch alive? I know that the blacks, take them half enlightened and ignorant, are more humane and merciful than the most enlightened and refined European that can be found in all the earth. Let no one say that I assert this because I am prejudiced on the side of my colour, and against the whites or Europeans. For what I write, I do it candidly, for my God and the good of both parties: Natural observations have taught me these things; there is a solemn awe in the hearts of the blacks, as it respects *murdering* men:* whereas the whites, (though they are great cowards) where they have the advantage, or think that there are any prospects of getting it, they murder all before them, in order to subject men to wretchedness and degradation under them. This is the natural result of pride and avarice. But I declare, the actions of this black woman are really insupportable. For my own part, I cannot think it was any thing but servile

* Which is the reason the whites take the advantage of us.

deceit, combined with the most gross ignorance: for we must remember that *humanity, kindness* and the *fear of the Lord*, does
not consist in protecting *devils*. Here is a set of wretches, who
had SIXTY of them in a gang, driving them around the country
like *brutes*, to dig up gold and silver for them, (which they will
get enough of yet.) Should the lives of such creatures be spared?
Are God and Mammon in league? What has the Lord to do with
a gang of desperate wretches, who go *sneaking about the country
like robbers*—light upon his people wherever they can get a
chance, binding them with chains and hand-cuffs, beat and murder them as they would *rattle-snakes?* Are they not the Lord's
enemies? Ought they not to be destroyed? Any person who
will save such wretches from destruction, is fighting against the
Lord, and will receive his just recompense. The black men acted
like *blockheads*. Why did they not make sure of the wretch? He
would have made sure of them, if he could. It is just the way
with black men—eight white men can frighten fifty of them;
whereas, if you can only get courage into the blacks, I do declare
it, that one good black man can put to death six white men; and
I give it as a fact, let twelve black men get well armed for battle,
and they will kill and put to flight fifty whites.—The reason is,
the blacks, once you get them started, they glory in death. The
whites have had us under them for more than three centuries,
murdering, and treating us like brutes; and, as Mr. Jefferson
wisely said, they have never *found us out*—they do not know,
indeed, that there is an unconquerable disposition in the breasts
of the blacks, which, when it is fully awakened and put in mo-
tion, will be subdued, only with the destruction of the animal
existence. Get the blacks started, and if you do not have a gang
of tigers and lions to deal with, I am a deceiver of the blacks and
of the whites. How sixty of them could let that wretch escape
unkilled, I cannot conceive—they will have to suffer as much
for the two whom, they secured, as if they had put one hundred
to death: if you commence, make sure work—do not trifle, for
they will not trifle with you—they want us for their slaves, and
think nothing of murdering us in order to subject us to that
wretched condition—therefore, if there is an *attempt* made by
us, kill or be killed. Now, I ask you, had you not rather be
killed than to be a slave to a tyrant, who takes the life of your

mother, wife, and dear little children? Look upon your mother, wife and children, and answer God Almighty; and believe this, that it is no more harm for you to kill a man, who is trying to kill you, than it is for you to take a drink of water when thirsty; in fact, the man who will stand still and let another murder him, is worse than an infidel, and, if he has common sense, ought not to be pitied. The actions of this deceitful and ignorant coloured woman, in saving the life of a desperate wretch, whose avaricious and cruel object was to drive her, and her companions in miseries, through the country like cattle, to make his fortune on their carcasses, are but too much like that of thousands of our brethren in these states: if any thing is whispered by one, which has any allusion to the melioration of their dreadful condition, they run and tell tyrants, that they may be enabled to keep them the longer in wretchedness and miseries. Oh! coloured people of these United States, I ask you, in the name of that God who made us, have we, in consequence of oppression, nearly lost the spirit of man, and, in no very trifling degree, adopted that of brutes? Do you answer, no?—I ask you, then, what set of men can you point me to, in all the world, who are so abjectly employed by their oppressors, as we are by our *natural enemies?* How can, Oh! how can those enemies but say that we and our children are not of the HUMAN FAMILY, but were made by our Creator to be an inheritance to them and theirs for ever? How can the slaveholders but say that they can bribe the best coloured person in the country, to sell his brethren for a trifling sum of money, and take that atrocity to confirm them in their avaricious opinion, that we were made to be slaves to them and their children? How could Mr. Jefferson but say, * "I advance it therefore as a suspicion only, that the blacks, whether originally a distinct race, or made distinct by time and circumstances, are *inferior* to the whites in the endowments both of body and mind?"—"It," says he, "is not against experience to suppose, that different species of the same genius, or varieties of the same species, may possess different qualifications." [Here, my brethren, listen to him.] ☞"Will not a lover of natural history, then, one who views the gradations in all the races of *animals* with the eye of philosophy, excuse an effort to keep those in the depart-

* See his Notes on Virginia, page 213.

ment of MAN as *distinct* as nature has formed them?"—I hope you will try to find out the meaning of this verse—its widest sense and all its bearings: whether you do or not, remember the whites do. This very verse, brethren, having emanated from Mr. Jefferson, a much greater philosopher the world never afforded, has in truth injured us more, and has been as great a barrier to our emancipation as any thing that has ever been advanced against us. I hope you will not let it pass unnoticed. He goes on further, and says: "This *unfortunate* difference of colour, and *perhaps* of *faculty,* is a powerful obstacle to the emancipation of these people. Many of their advocates, while they wish to vindicate the liberty of human nature are anxious also to preserve its *dignity* and *beauty.* Some of these, embarrassed by the question, 'What further is to be done with them?' join themselves in opposition with those who are actuated by sordid avarice only." Now I ask you candidly, my suffering brethren in time, who are candidates for the eternal worlds, how could Mr. Jefferson but have given the world these remarks respecting us, when we are so submissive to them, and so much servile deceit prevail among ourselves—when we so *meanly* submit to their murderous lashes, to which neither the Indians nor any other people under Heaven would submit? No, they would die to a man, before they would suffer such things from men who are no better than themselves, and *perhaps not so good.* Yes, how can our friends but be embarrassed, as Mr. Jefferson says, by the question, "What further is to be done with these people?" For while they are working for our emancipation, we are, by our treachery, wickedness and deceit, working against ourselves and our children—helping ours, and the enemies of God, to keep us and our dear little children in their infernal chains of slavery! ! ! Indeed, our friends cannot but relapse and join themselves "with those who are actuated by *sordid avarice* only! ! ! !" For my own part, I am glad Mr. Jefferson has advanced his positions for your sake; for you will either have to contradict or confirm him by your own actions, and not by what our friends have said or done for us; for those things are other men's labours, and do not satisfy the Americans, who are waiting for us to prove to them ourselves, that we are MEN, before they will be willing to admit the fact; for I pledge you my sacred word of honour, that Mr. Jefferson's remarks respecting us, have sunk deep into the hearts of millions of the whites, and never will be removed this side of eternity.—For how can they, when we are confirming him every day, by our *groveling submissions* and *treachery?* I aver, that when I look over these United States of America, and the world, and see the ignorant deceptions and consequent wretchedness of my brethren, I am brought oftimes solemnly to a stand, and in the midst of my reflections I exclaim to my God, "Lord didst thou make us to be slaves to our brethren, the whites?" But when I reflect that God is just, and that millions of my wretched brethren would meet death with glory—yea, more, would plunge into the very mouths of cannons and be torn into particles as minute as the atoms which compose the elements of the earth, in preference to a mean submission to the lash of tyrants, I am with streaming eyes, compelled to shrink back into nothingness before my Maker, and exclaim again, thy will be done, O Lord God Almighty.

Men of colour, who are also of sense, for you particularly is my APPEAL designed. Our more ignorant brethren are not able to penetrate its value. I call upon you therefore to cast your eyes upon the wretchedness of your brethren, and to do your utmost to enlighten them—*go to work and enlighten your brethren!*—Let the Lord see you doing what you can to rescue them and yourselves from degradation. Do any of you say that you and your family are free and happy, and what have you to do with the wretched slaves and other people? So can I say, for I enjoy as much freedom as any of you, if I am not quite as well off as the best of you. Look into our freedom and happiness, and see of what kind they are composed! ! They are of the very lowest kind—they are the very *dregs!*—they are the most servile and abject kind, that ever a people was in possession of! If any of you wish to know how FREE you are, let one of you start and go through the southern and western States of this country, and unless you travel as a slave to a white man (a servant is a *slave* to the man whom he serves) or have your free papers, (which if you are not careful they will get from you) if they do not take you up and put you in jail, and if you cannot give good evidence of your freedom, sell you into eternal slavery, I am not a living man: or any man of colour, immaterial who he is, or where he

came from, if he is not *the fourth from the negro race!* ! (as we are called) the white Christians of America will serve him the same they will sink him into wretchedness and degradation for ever while he lives. And yet some of you have the hardihood to say that you are free and happy! May God have mercy on your freedom and happiness! ! I met a coloured man in the street a short time since, with a string of boots on his shoulders; we fell into conversation, and in course of which, I said to him, what a miserable set of people we are! He asked, why?—Said I, we are so subjected under the whites, that we cannot obtain the comforts of life, but by cleaning their boots and shoes, old clothes, waiting on them, shaving them &c. Said he, (with the boots on his shoulders) "I am completely happy! ! ! I never want to live any better or happier than when I can get a plenty of boots and shoes to clean! ! !" Oh! how can those who are actuated by avarice only, but think, that our Creator made us to be an inheritance to them for ever, when they see that our greatest glory is centered in such mean and low objects? Understand me, brethren, I do not mean to speak against the occupations by which we acquire enough and sometimes scarcely that, to render ourselves and families comfortable through life. I am subjected to the same inconvenience, as you all.—My objections are, to our *glorying* and being *happy* in such low employments; for if we are men, we ought to be thankful to the Lord for the past, and for the future. Be looking forward with thankful hearts to higher attainments than *wielding the razor* and *cleaning boots and shoes.* The man whose aspirations are not *above,* and even *below* these, is indeed, ignorant and wretched enough. I advanced it therefore to you, not as a *problematical,* but as an unshaken and for ever immovable *fact,* that your full glory and happiness, as well as all other coloured people under Heaven, shall never be fully consummated, but with the *entire emancipation of your enslaved brethren all over the world.* You may therefore, go to work and do what you can to rescue, or join in with tyrants to oppress them and yourselves, until the Lord shall come upon you all like a thief in the night. For I believe it is the will of the Lord that our greatest happiness shall consist in working for the salvation of our whole body. When this is accomplished a burst of glory will shine upon you, which will indeed astonish you

and the world. Do any of you say this never will be done? I assure you that God will accomplish it—if nothing else will answer, he will hurl tyrants and devils into *atoms* and make way for his people. But O my brethren! I say unto you again, you must go to work and prepare the way of the Lord.

There is a great work for you to do, as trifling as some of you may think of it. You have to prove to the Americans and the world, that we are MEN, and not *brutes,* as we have been represented, and by millions treated. Remember, to let the aim of your labours among your brethren, and particularly the youths, be the dissemination of education and religion.* It is lamentable, that many of our children go to school, from four until they are eight or ten, and sometimes fifteen years of age, and leave school knowing but a little more about the grammar of their language than a horse does about handling a musket—and not a few of them are really so ignorant, that they are unable to answer a person correctly, general questions in geography, and to hear them read, would only be to disgust a man who has a taste for reading; which, to do well, as trifling as it may appear to some, (to the ignorant in particular) is a great part of learning. Some few of them, may make out to scribble tolerably well, over a half sheet of paper, which I believe has hitherto been a powerful obstacle in our way, to keep us from acquiring knowledge. An ignorant father, who knows no more than what nature has taught him, together with what little he acquires by the senses of hearing and seeing, finding his son able to write a neat hand, sets it down for granted that he has as good learning as any body; the young, ignorant gump, hearing his father or mother, who perhaps may be ten times more ignorant, in point of literature, than himself, extolling his learning, struts about, in the full assurance, that his attainments in literature are suffi-

* Never mind what the ignorant ones among us may say, many of whom when you speak to them for their good, and try to enlighten their minds, laugh at you, and perhaps tell you plump to your face, that they want no instruction from you or any other Niger, and all such aggravating language. Now if you are a man of understanding and sound sense, I conjure you in the name of the Lord, and of all that is good, to impute their actions to ignorance, and wink at their follies, and do your very best to get around them some way or other, for remember they are your brethren; and I declare to you that it is for your interests to teach and enlighten them.

cient to take him through the world, when, in fact, he has scarcely any learning at all! ! ! !

I promiscuously fell in conversation once, with an elderly coloured man on the topics of education, and of the great prevalency of ignorance among us: Said he, "I know that our people are very ignorant but my son has a good education: I spent a great deal of money on his education: he can write as well as any white man, and I assure you that no one can fool him," &c. Said I, what else can your son do, besides writing a good hand? Can he post a set of books in a mercantile manner? Can he write a neat piece of composition in prose or in verse? To these interrogations he answered in the negative. Said I, did your son learn, while he was at school, the width and depth of English Grammar? To which he also replied in the negative, telling me his son did not learn those things. Your son, said I, then, has hardly any learning at all—he is almost as ignorant, and more so, than many of those who never went to school one day in all their lives. My friend got a little put out, and so walking off, said that his son could write as well as any white man. Most of the coloured people, when they speak of the education of one among us who can write a neat hand, and who perhaps knows nothing but to scribble and puff pretty fair on a small scrap of paper, immaterial whether his words are grammatical, or spelt correctly, or not; if it only looks beautiful, they say he has as good an education as any white man—he can write as well as any white man, &c. The poor, ignorant creature, hearing, this, he is ashamed, forever after, to let any person see him humbling himself to another for knowledge but going about trying to deceive those who are more ignorant than himself, he at last falls an ignorant victim to death in wretchedness. I pray that the Lord may undeceive my ignorant brethren, and permit them to throw away pretensions, and seek after the substance of learning. I would crawl on my hands and knees through mud and mire, to the feet of a learned man, where I would sit and humbly supplicate him to instil into me, that which neither devils nor tyrants could remove, only with my life—for coloured people to acquire learning in this country, makes tyrants quake and tremble on their sandy foundation.

Why, what is the matter? Why, they know that their infernal deeds of cruelty will be made known to the world. Do you suppose one man of good sense and learning would submit himself, his father, mother, wife and children, to be slaves to a wretched man like himself, who, instead of compensating him for his labours, chains, hand-cuffs and beats him and family almost to death, leaving life enough in them, however, to work for, and call him master? No! no! he would cut his devilish throat from ear to ear, and well do slave-holders know it. The bare name of educating the coloured people, scares our cruel oppressors almost to death. But if they do not have enough to be frightened for yet, it will be, because they can always keep us ignorant, and because God approbates their cruelties, with which they have been for centuries murdering us. The whites shall have enough of the blacks, yet, as true as God sits on his throne in Heaven.

Some of our brethren are so very full of learning, that you cannot mention any thing to them which they do not know better than yourself! !—nothing is strange to them! !—they knew every thing years ago!—if any thing should be mentioned in company where they are, immaterial how important it is respecting us or the world, if they had not divulged it; they make light of it, and affect to have known it long before it was mentioned and try to make all in the room, or wherever you may be, believe that your conversation is nothing! !—not worth hearing! All this is the result of ignorance and ill-breeding; for a man of good-breeding, sense and penetration, if he had heard a subject told twenty times over, and should happen to be in company where one should commence telling it again, he would wait with patience on its narrator, and see if he would tell it as it was told in his presence before—paying the most strict attention to what is said, to see if any more light will be thrown on the subject: for all men are not gifted alike in telling, or even hearing the most simple narration. These ignorant, vicious, and wretched men, contribute almost as much injury to our body as tyrants themselves, by doing so much for the promotion of ignorance amongst us; for they, making such pretensions to knowledge, such of our youth as are seeking after knowledge, and can get access to them, take them as criterions to go by, who will lead them into a channel, where, unless the Lord blesses them with the privilege of seeing their folly, they will be irretrievably lost forever, while in time! ! !

I must close this article by relating the very heart-rending fact, that I have examined school-boys and young men of colour in different parts of the country, in the most simple parts of Murray's English Grammar, and not more than one in thirty was able to give a correct answer to my interrogations. If any one contradicts me, let him step out of his door into the streets of Boston, New-York, Philadelphia, or Baltimore, (no use to mention any other, for the Christians are too charitable further south or west!)—I say, let him who disputes me, step out of his door into the streets of either of those four cities, and promiscuously collect one hundred school-boys, or young men of colour, *who have been to school,* and who are considered by the coloured people to have received an excellent education, because, perhaps, some of them can write a good hand, but who, notwithstanding their neat writing, may be almost as ignorant, in comparison, as a horse.—And, I say it, he will hardly find (in this enlightened day, and in the midst of this *charitable* people) five in one hundred, who, are able to correct the false grammar of their language.—The cause of this almost universal ignorance among us, I appeal to our schoolmasters to declare. Here is a fact, which I this very minute take from the mouth of a young coloured man, who has been to school in this state (Massachusetts) nearly nine years, and who knows grammar this day, *nearly* as well as he did the day he first entered the schoolhouse, under a white master. This young man says: "My master would never allow me to study grammar." I asked him, why? "The school committee," said he "forbid the coloured children learning grammar—they would not allow any but the white children to study grammar." It is a notorious fact, that the major part of the white Americans, have, ever since we have been among them, tried to keep us ignorant, and make us believe that God made us and our children to be slaves to them and theirs. *Oh! my God, have mercy on Christian Americans! ! !*

ARTICLE III.

Religion, my brethren, is a substance of deep consideration among all nations of the earth. The Pagans have a kind, as well as the Mahometans, the Jews and the Christians. But pure and undefiled religion, such as was preached by Jesus Christ and his apostles, is hard to be found in all the earth. God, through his instrument, Moses, handed a dispensation of his Divine will, to the children of Israel after they had left Egypt for the land of Canaan or of Promise, who through hypocrisy, oppression and unbelief, departed from the faith.—He then, by his apostles, handed a dispensation of his, together with the will of Jesus Christ, to the Europeans in Europe, who, in open violation of which, have made *merchandise* of us, and it does appear as though they take this very dispensation to aid them in their *infernal* depredations upon us. Indeed, the way in which religion was and is conducted by the Europeans and their descendants, one might believe it was a plan fabricated by themselves and the *devils* to oppress us. But hark! My master has taught me better than to believe it—he has taught me that his gospel as it was preached by himself and his apostles remains the same, notwithstanding Europe has tried to mingle blood and opression with it.

It is well known to the Christian world, that Bartholomew Las Casas, that very very notoriously avaricious Catholic priest or preacher, and adventurer with Columbus in his second voyage,

35

proposed to his countrymen, the Spaniards in Hispaniola to import the Africans from the Portuguese settlement in Africa, to dig up gold and silver, and work their plantations for them, to effect which, he made a voyage thence to Spain, and opened the subject to his master, Ferdinand then in declining health, who listened to the plan: but who died soon after, and left it in the hand of his successor, Charles V.* This wretch, ("Las Casas, the Preacher,") succeeded so well in his plans of oppression, that in 1503, the first blacks had been imported into the new world. Elated with this success, and stimulated by sordid avarice only, he importuned Charles V. in 1511, to grant permission to a Flemish merchant, to import 4000 blacks at one time.† Thus we see, through the instrumentality of a pretended preacher of the gospel of Jesus Christ our common master, our wretchedness first commenced in America—where it has been continued from 1503, to this day, 1829. A period of three hundred and twenty-six years. But two hundred and nine, from 1620 [1619]—when twenty of our fathers were brought into Jamestown, Virginia, by a Dutch man of war, and sold off like brutes to the highest bidders; and there is not a doubt in my mind, but that tyrants are in hope to perpetuate our miseries under them and their children until the final consumation of all things.—But if they do not get dreadfully deceived, it will be because God has forgotten them.

The Pagans, Jews and Mahometans try to make proselytes to their religions, and whatever human beings adopt their religions

* See Butler's History of the United States, vol. 1, page 24.—See also, page 25. [The citation is to Frederick Butler, *A Complete History of the United States of America, Embracing the Whole Period from the Discovery of North America, down to the Year 1820.* 3 vols., Hartford, 1821. Ed.]

† It is not unworthy of remark, that the Portuguese and Spaniards, were among, if not the very first Nations upon Earth, about three hundred and fifty or sixty years ago—But see what those *Christians* have come to now in consequence of afflicting our fathers and us, who have never molested, or disturbed them or any other of the white *Christians,* but have they received one quarter of what the Lord will yet bring upon them, for the murders they have inflicted upon us?—They have had, and in some degree have now, sweet times on our blood and groans, the time however, of bitterness have sometime since commenced with them.—There is a God the Maker and preserver of all things, who will as sure as the world exists, give all his creatures their just recompense of reward in this and in the world to come,—we may fool or deceive, and keep each other in the most profound ignorance, beat murder and keep each other out of what is our lawful rights, or the rights of man, yet it is impossible for us to deceive or escape the Lord Almighty.

they extend to them their protection. But Christian Americans, not only hinder their fellow creatures, the Africans, but thousands of them *will absolutely beat a coloured person nearly to death, if they catch him on his knees, supplicating the throne of grace.* This barbarous cruelty was by all the heathen nations of antiquity, and is by the Pagans, Jews and Mahometans of the present day, left entirely to Christian Americans to inflict on the Africans and their descendants, that their cup which is nearly full may be completed. I have known tyrants or usurpers of human liberty in different parts of this country to take their fellow creatures, the coloured people, and beat them until they would scarcely leave life in them; what for? Why they say "The black devils had the audacity to be found *making prayers and supplications to the God who made them! ! ! !*" Yes, I have known small collections of coloured people to have convened together, for no other purpose than to worship God Almighty, in spirit and in truth, to the best of their knowledge; when tyrants, calling themselves *patrols,* would also convene and wait almost in breathless silence for the poor coloured people to commence singing and praying to the Lord our God, as soon as they had commenced, the wretches would burst in upon them and drag them out and commence beating them as they would rattle-snakes—many of whom, they would beat so unmercifully, that they would hardly be able to crawl for weeks and sometimes for months. Yet the American ministers send out missionaries to convert the heathen, while they keep us and our children sunk at their feet in the most abject ignorance and wretchedness that ever a people was afflicted with since the world began. Will the Lord suffer this people to proceed much longer? Will he not stop them in their career? Does he regard the heathens abroad, more than the heathens among the Americans? Surely the Americans must believe that God is partial, notwithstanding his Apostle Peter, declared before Cornelius and others that he has no respect to persons, but in every nation he that feareth God and worketh righteousness is accepted with him.—"The word," said he, "which God sent unto the children of Israel, preaching peace, by Jesus Christ, (he is Lord of all."*) Have not the Americans the Bible in their hands?

* See Acts of the Apostles, chap. x. v.—25—27. [The citation should be to Acts 10:36. Ed.]

Do they believe it? Surely they do not. See how they treat us in
open violation of the Bible! I They no doubt will be greatly of-
fended with me, but if God does not awaken them, it will be, because they are superior to other men, as they have represented
themselves to be. Our divine Lord and Master said, "all things
whatsoever ye would that men should do unto you, do ye even
so unto them." But an American minister, with the Bible in his
hand, holds us and our children in the most abject slavery and
wretchedness. Now I ask them, would they like for us to hold
them and their children in abject slavery and wretchedness? No,
says one, that never can be done—you are too abject and ignorant to do it—you are not men—you were made to be slaves
to us, to dig up gold and silver for us and our children. Know
this, my dear sirs, that although you treat us and our children
now, as you do your domestic beast—yet the final result of all
future events are known but to God Almighty alone, who rules in
the armies of heaven and among the inhabitants of the earth, and
who dethrones one earthly king and sits up another, as it seem-
eth good in his holy sight. We may attribute these vicissitudes to
what we please, but the God of armies and of justice rules in
heaven and in earth, and the whole American people shall see and
know it yet, to their satisfaction. I have known pretended
preachers of the gospel of my Master, who not only held us as
their natural inheritance, but treated us with as much rigor as
any Infidel or Deist in the world—just as though they were in-
tent only on taking our blood and groans to glorify the Lord
Jesus Christ. The wicked and ungodly, seeing their preachers
treat us with so much cruelty, they say: our preachers, who must
be right, if any body are, treat them like brutes, and why cannot
we?—They think it is no harm to keep them in slavery and put
the whip to them, and why cannot we do the same!—They being
preachers of the gospel of Jesus Christ, if it were any harm, they
would surely preach against their oppression and do their utmost
to erase it from the country; not only in one or two cities, but
one continual cry would be raised in all parts of this confederacy,
and would cease only with the complete overthrow of the system
of slavery, in every part of the country. But how far the American preachers are from preaching against slavery and oppression,

which have carried their country to the brink of a precipice; to save them from plunging down the side of which, will hardly be affected, will appear in the sequel of this paragraph, which I shall narrate just as it transpired. I remember a Camp Meeting in South Carolina, for which I embarked in a Steam Boat at Charleston, and having been five or six hours on the water, we at last arrived at the place of hearing, where was a very great concourse of people, who were no doubt, collected together to hear the word of God, (that some had collected barely as spectators to the scene, I will not here pretend to doubt, however, that is left to themselves and their God.) Myself and boat companions, having been there a little while, we were all called up to hear; I among the rest went up and took my seat—being seated, I fixed myself in a complete position to hear the word of my Saviour and to receive such as I thought was authenticated by the Holy Scriptures; but to my no ordinary astonishment, our Reverend gentleman got up and told us (coloured people) that slaves must be obedient to their masters—must do their duty to their masters or be whipped —the whip was made for the backs of fools, &c. Here I pause for a moment, to give the world time to consider what was my surprise, to hear such preaching from a minister of my Master, whose very gospel is that of peace and not of blood and whips, as this pretended preacher tried to make us believe. What the American preachers can think of us, I aver this day before my God, I have never been able to define. They have newspapers and monthly periodicals, which they receive in continual succession, but on the pages of which, you will scarcely ever find a paragraph respecting slavery, which is ten thousand times more injurious to this country than all the other evils put together; and which will be the final overthrow of its government, unless something is very speedily done; for their cup is nearly full.—Perhaps they will laugh at or make light of this; but I tell you Americans ! that unless you speedily alter your course, *you* and your *Country are gone! ! ! ! ! !* For God Almighty will tear up the very face of the earth! ! ! Will not that very remarkable passage of Scripture be fulfilled on Christian Americans? Hear it Americans! ! "He that is unjust, let him be unjust still:—and he which is filthy, let him be filthy still: and he that is righteous, let him be righteous still: and he that is holy, let him be holy still." * I hope that the Americans may hear, but I am afraid that they have done us so much injury, and are so firm in the belief that our Creator made us to be an inheritance to them for ever, that their hearts will be hardened, so that their destruction may be sure. This language, perhaps is too harsh for the American's delicate ears. But Oh Americans! Americans! ! I warn you in the name of the Lord, (whether you will hear, or forbear,) to repent and reform, or you are ruined! ! ! Do you think that our blood is hidden from the Lord, because you can hide it from the rest of the world, by sending out missionaries, and by your charitable deeds to the Greeks, Irish, &c.? Will he not publish your secret crimes on the house top? Even here in Boston, pride and prejudice have got to such a pitch, that in the very houses erected to the Lord, they have built little places for the reception of coloured people, where they must sit during meeting, or keep away from the house of God, and the preachers say nothing about it—much less go into the hedges and highways seeking the lost sheep of the house of Israel, and try to bring them in to their Lord and Master. There are not a more wretched, ignorant, miserable, and abject set of beings in all the world, than the blacks in the Southern and Western sections of this country, under tyrants and devils. The preachers of America cannot see them, but they can send out missionaries to convert the heathens, notwithstanding. Americans! unless you speedily alter your course of proceeding, if God Almighty does not stop you, I say it in his name, that you may go on and do as you please for ever, both in time and eternity—never fear any evil at all! ! ! ! ! ! ! !

☞ ADDITION.—The preachers and people of the United States form societies against Free Masonry and Intemperance, and write against Sabbath breaking, Sabbath mails, Infidelity, &c. &c. But the fountain head,† compared with which, all those other evils are comparatively nothing, and from the bloody and murderous head of which, they receive no trifling support, is hardly noticed by the Americans. This is a fair illustration of the state of so-

* See Revelation, chap. xxii. 11.
† Slavery and oppression. [The allusion to Free Masonry refers to the furor following the threatened revelation of Masonic secrets by William Morgan in 1826, and Morgan's subsequent murder. Ed.]

ciety in this country—it shows what a bearing *avarice* has upon a people, when they are nearly given up by the Lord to a hard heart and a reprobate mind, in consequence of afflicting their fellow creatures. God suffers some to go on until they are ruined for ever! ! ! ! ! Will it be the case with the whites of the United States of America?—We hope not—we would not wish to see them destroyed notwithstanding, they have and do now treat us more cruel than any people have treated another, on this earth since it came from the hands of its Creator (with the exceptions of the French and the Dutch, they treat us nearly as bad as the Americans of the United States.) The will of God must however, in spite of us, *be done.*

The English are the best friends the coloured people have upon earth. Though they have oppressed us a little and have colonies now in the West Indies, which oppress us *sorely.*—Yet notwithstanding they (the English) have done one hundred times more for the melioration of our condition, than all the other nations of the earth put together. The blacks cannot but respect the English as a nation, notwithstanding they have treated us a little cruel.

There is no intelligent *black man* who knows any thing, but esteems a real Englishman, let him see him in what part of the world he will—for they are the greatest benefactors we have upon earth. We have here and there, in other nations, good friends. But as a nation, the English are our friends.

How can the preachers and people of America believe the Bible? Does it teach them any distinction on account of a man's colour? Hearken, Americans! to the injunctions of our Lord and Master, to his humble followers.

* "And Jesus came and spake unto them, saying, all power is given unto me in Heaven and in earth.

"Go ye, therefore, and teach all nations, baptizing them in the name of the Father, and of the Son, and of the Holy Ghost.

"Teaching them to observe all things whatsoever I have commanded you; and lo, I am with you alway, even unto the end of the world. Amen."

* See St. Matthew's Gospel, chap. xxviii. 18, 19, 20. After Jesus was risen from the dead.

I declare, that the very face of these injunctions appear to be of God and not of man. They do not show the slightest degree of distinction. "Go ye therefore," (says my divine Master) "and teach all nations," (or in other words, all people) "baptizing them in the name of the Father, and of the Son, and of the Holy Ghost." Do you understand the above, Americans? We are a people, notwithstanding many of you doubt it. You have the Bible in your hands, with this very injunction.—Have you been to Africa, teaching the inhabitants thereof the words of the Lord Jesus? "Baptizing them in the name of the Father, and of the Son and of the Holy Ghost." Have you not, on the contrary, entered among us, and learnt us the art of throat-cutting, by setting us to fight, one against another, to take each other as prisoners of war, and sell to you for small bits of calicoes, old swords, knives, &c. to make slaves for you and your children? This being done, have you not brought us among you, in chains and hand-cuffs, like brutes, and treated us with all the cruelties and rigour your ingenuity could invent, consistent with the laws of your country, which (for the blacks) are tyrannical enough? Can the American preachers appeal unto God, the Maker and Searcher of hearts, and tell him, with the Bible in their hands, that they make no distinction on account of men's colour? Can they say, O God! thou knowest all things—thou knowest that we make no distinction between thy creatures, to whom we have to preach thy Word? Let them answer the Lord; and if they cannot do it in the affirmative, have they not departed from the Lord Jesus Christ, their master? But some may say, that they never had, or were in possession of religion, which made no distinction, and of course they could not have departed from it. I ask you then, in the name of the Lord, of what kind can your religion be? Can it be that which was preached by our Lord Jesus Christ from Heaven? I believe you cannot be so wicked as to tell him that his Gospel was that of *distinction*. What can the American preachers and people take God to be? Do they believe his words? If they do, do they believe that he will be mocked? Or do they believe, because they are whites and we blacks, that God will have respect to them? Did not God make us all as it seemed best to himself? What right, then, has one of us, to despise another, and to treat him cruel, on account of his colour, which none, but the God who made it can alter? Can there be a greater absurdity in nature, and particularly in a free republican country? But the Americans, having introduced slavery among them, their hearts have become almost seared, as with an hot iron, and God has nearly given them up to believe a lie in preference to the truth! ! ! And I am awfully afraid that pride, prejudice, avarice and blood, will, before long prove the final ruin of this happy republic, or land of *liberty! ! ! !* Can any thing be a greater mockery of religion than the way in which it is conducted by the Americans? It appears as though they are bent only on daring God Almighty to do his best—they chain and handcuff us and our children and drive us around the country like brutes, and go into the house of the God of justice to return him thanks for having aided them in their infernal cruelties inflicted upon us. Will the Lord suffer this people to go on much longer, taking his holy name in vain? Will he not stop them, PREACHERS and all? O Americans! Americans! ! I call God—I call angels—I call men, to witness, that your DESTRUCTION *is at hand,* and will be speedily consummated unless you REPENT.

ARTICLE IV.

OUR WRETCHEDNESS IN CONSEQUENCE OF THE
COLONIZING PLAN.

My dearly beloved brethren:—This is a scheme on which so many able writers, together with that very judicious coloured Baltimorean,* have commented, that I feel my delicacy about touching it. But as I am compelled to do the will of my Master, I declare, I will give you my sentiments upon it.—Previous, however, to giving my sentiments, either for or against it, I shall give that of Mr. Henry Clay, together with that of Mr. Elias B. Caldwell, Esq. of the District of Columbia, as extracted from the' National Intelligencer, by Dr. Torrey, author of a series of "Essays on Morals, and the Diffusion of Useful Knowledge."

At a meeting which was convened in the District of Columbia, for the express purpose of agitating the subject of colonizing us in some part of the world, Mr. Clay was called to the chair, and having been seated a little while, he rose and spake, in substance, as follows: says he—† "That class of the mixt population of our

* [There were many Baltimore Negroes who commented, both favorably and otherwise, on the Colonization scheme, including many colored ministers such as William Cornish, Robert Cowley, James Deaver, and Remus Harvey. It is most likely, however, that Walker was referring to Hezekiah Grice, who, a few months before the *Appeal* was written, had sought to form a Liberian Trade Association, with capital supplied by free Negroes.]

† See Dr. Torrey's Portraiture of Domestic Slavery in the United States, pages 85, 86. [The report of the meeting from which these quotations are taken is in the *National Intelligencer*, Dec. 24, 1816. Ed.]

country [coloured people] was peculiarly situated; they neither enjoyed the immunities of freemen, nor were they subjected to the incapacities of slaves, but partook, in some degree, of the qualities of both. From their condition, and the unconquerable prejudices resulting from their colour, they never could amalgamate with the free whites of this country. It was desirable, therefore, as it respected them, and the residue of the population of the country, to drain them off. Various schemes of colonization had been thought of, and a part of our continent, it was supposed by some, might furnish a suitable establishment for them. But, for his part, Mr. C. said, he had a decided preference for some part of the Coast of Africa. There ample provision might be made for the colony itself, and it might be rendered instrumental to the introduction into that extensive quarter of the globe, of the arts, civilization, and Christianity." [Here I ask Mr. Clay, what kind of Christianity? Did he mean such as they have among the Americans—distinction, whip, blood and oppression? I pray the Lord Jesus Christ to forbid it.] "There," said he, "was a peculiar, a moral fitness, in restoring them to the land of their fathers, and if instead of the evils and sufferings which we had been the innocent cause of inflicting upon the inhabitants of Africa, we can transmit to her the blessings of our arts, our civilization, and our religion. May we not hope that America will extinguish a great portion of that moral debt which she has contracted to that unfortunate continent? Can there be a nobler cause than that which, whilst it proposes," &c. * * * * * * * [you know what this means.] "contemplates the spreading of the arts of civilized life, and the possible redemption from ignorance and barbarism of a benighted quarter of the globe?"

Before I proceed any further, I solicit your notice, brethren, to the foregoing part of Mr. Clay's speech, in which he says, (☞look above) "and if, instead of the evils and sufferings, which we had been the innocent cause of inflicting," &c.—What this very learned statesman could have been thinking about, when he said in his speech, "we had been the innocent cause of inflicting," &c., I have never been able to conceive. Are Mr. Clay and the rest of the Americans, innocent of the blood and groans of our fathers and us, their children?—Every individual may plead innocence, if he pleases, but God will, before long, separate the

innocent from the guilty, unless something is speedily done—
which I suppose will hardly be, so that their destruction may be
sure. Oh Americans! let me tell you, in the name of the Lord,
it will be good for you, if you listen to the voice of the Holy
Ghost, but if you do not, you are ruined! ! ! Some of you are
good men; but the will of my God must be done. Those avaricious
and ungodly tyrants among you, I am awfully afraid will drag
down the vengeance of God upon you. When God Almighty
commences his battle on the continent of America, for the oppression of his people, tyrants will wish they never were born.

But to return to Mr. Clay, whence I digressed. He says, "It
was proper and necessary distinctly to state, that he understood
it constituted no part of the object of this meeting, to touch or
agitate in the slightest degree, a delicate question, connected with
another portion of the coloured population of our country. It
was not proposed to deliberate upon or consider at all, any
question of emancipation, or that which was connected with the
abolition of slavery. It was upon that condition alone, he was
sure, that many gentlemen from the South and the West, whom
he saw present, had attended, or could be expected to co-operate.
It was upon that condition only, that he himself had attended."
—That is to say, to fix a plan to get those of the coloured people,
who are said to be free, away from among those of our brethren
whom they unjustly hold in bondage, so that they may be enabled
to keep them the more secure in ignorance and wretchedness, to
support them and their children, and consequently they would
have the more obedient slaves. For if the free are allowed to
stay among the slaves, they will have intercourse together, and,
of course, the free will learn the slaves *bad habits*, by teaching
them that they are MEN, as well as other people, and certainly
ought and *must* be FREE.

I presume, that every intelligent man of colour must have
some idea of Mr. Henry Clay, originally of Virginia, but now of
Kentucky; they know too, perhaps, whether he is a friend, or a
foe to the coloured citizens of this country, and of the world.
This gentleman, according to his own words, had been highly
favoured and blessed of the Lord, though he did not acknowledge
it; but, to the contrary, he acknowledged men, for all the blessings with which God had favoured him. At a public dinner, given

him at Fowler's Garden, Lexington, Kentucky, he delivered a public speech to a very large concourse of people—in the concluding clause of which, he says, "And now, my friends and fellow citizens, I cannot part from you, on possibly the last occasion of my ever publicly addressing you, without reiterating the expression of my thanks, from a heart overflowing with gratitude. I came among you, now more than thirty years ago, an orphan boy, pennyless, a stranger to you all, without friends, without the favour of the great, you took me up, cherished me, protected me, honoured me, you have constantly poured upon me a bold and unabated stream of innumerable favours, time which wears out every thing has increased and strengthened your affection for me. When I seemed deserted by almost the whole world, and assailed by almost every tongue, and pen, and press, you have fearlessly and manfully stood by me, with unsurpassed zeal and undiminished friendship. When I felt as if I should sink beneath the storm of abuse and detraction, which was violently raging around me, I have found myself upheld and sustained by your encouraging voices and approving smiles. I have doubtless, committed many faults and indiscretions, over which you have thrown the broad mantle of your charity. But I can say, and in the presence of God and in this assembled multitude, I will say, that I have honestly and faithfully served my country—that I have never wronged it—and that, however unprepared, I lament that I am to appear in the Divine presence on other accounts, I invoke the stern justice of his judgment on my public conduct, without the slightest apprehension of his displeasure."

Hearken to this Statesman indeed, but no philanthropist, whom God sent into Kentucky, an orphan boy, pennyless, and friendless, where he not only gave him a plenty of friends and the comforts of life, but raised him almost to the very highest honour in the nation, where his great talents, with which the Lord has been pleased to bless him, has gained for him the affection of a great portion of the people with whom he had to do. But what has this gentleman done for the Lord, after having done so much for him? The Lord has a suffering people, whose moans and groans at his feet for deliverance from oppression and wretchedness, pierce the very throne of Heaven, and call loudly on the God of Justice, to be revenged. Now, what this gentleman, who is so highly favoured of the Lord, has done to liberate those miserable victims of oppression, shall appear before the world, by his letters to Mr. Gallatin, Envoy Extraordinary and Minister Plenipotentiary to Great Britain, dated June 19, 1826.—Though Mr. Clay was writing for the States, yet nevertheless, it appears, from the very face of his letters to that gentleman, that he was as anxious, if not more so, to get those free people and sink them into wretchedness, as his constituents, for whom he wrote.

The Americans of North and of South America, including the West India Islands—no trifling portion of whom were, for stealing, murdering, &c. compelled to flee from Europe, to save their necks or banishment, have effected their escape to this continent, where God blessed them with all the comforts of life— He gave them a plenty of every thing calculated to do them good—not satisfied with this, however, they wanted slaves, and wanted us for their slaves, who belong to the Holy Ghost, and no other, who we shall have to serve instead of tyrants.—I say, the Americans want us, the property of the Holy Ghost, to serve them. But there is a day fast approaching, when (unless there is a universal repentance on the part of the whites, which will scarcely take place, they have got to be so hardened in conse- quence of our blood, and so wise in their own conceit.) To be plain and candid with you, Americans! I say that the day is fast approaching, when there will be a greater time on the con- tinent of America, than ever was witnessed upon this earth, since it came from the hand of its Creator. Some of you have done us so much injury, that you will never be able to repent.— Your cup must be filled.—You want us for your slaves, and shall have enough of us—God is just, *who will give you your fill of us*. But Mr. Henry Clay, speaking to Mr. Gallatin, respecting col- oured people, who had effected their escape from the U. States (or to them *hell upon earth! ! !*) to the hospitable shores of Canada,* from whence it would cause more than the lives of the Americans to get them, to plunge into wretchedness—he says: "The General Assembly of Kentucky, one of the states which is most affected by the escape of slaves into Upper Canada, has again, at their session which has just terminated, invoked the

* Among the English, our real friends and benefactors.

interposition of the General Government. In the treaty which has been recently concluded with the United Mexican States, and which is now under the consideration of the Senate, provision is made for the restoration of fugitive slaves. As it appears from your statements of what passed on that subject, with the British Plenipotentiaries, that they admitted the correctness of the principle of restoration, it is hoped that you will be able to succeed in making satisfactory arrangements."

There are a series of these letters, all of which are to the same amount; some however, presenting a face more of his own responsibility. I wonder what would this gentleman think, if the Lord should give him among the rest of his blessings enough of slaves? Could he blame any other being but himself? Do we not belong to the Holy Ghost? What business has he or any body else, to be sending letters about the world respecting us? Can we not go where we want to, as well as other people, only if we obey the voice of the Holy Ghost? This gentleman, (Mr. Henry Clay) not only took an active part in this colonizing plan, but was absolutely chairman of a meeting held at Washington, the 21st day of December 1816,* to agitate the subject of colonizing us in Africa.—Now I appeal and ask every citizen of these United States and of the world, both *white* and *black*, who has any knowledge of Mr. Clay's public labor for these States—I want you candidly to answer the Lord, who sees the secrets of our hearts.—Do you believe that Mr. Henry Clay, late Secretary of State, and now in Kentucky, is a friend to the blacks, further, than his personal interest extends? Is it not his greatest object and glory upon earth, to sink us into miseries and wretchedness by making slaves of us, to work his plantation to enrich him and his family? Does he care a pinch of snuff about Africa—whether it remains a land of Pagans and of blood, or of Christians, so long as he gets enough of her sons and daughters to dig up gold and silver for him? If he had no slaves, and could obtain them in no other way if it were not, repugnant to the laws of his country, which prohibit the importation of slaves (which act was, indeed, more through apprehension than humanity) would he not try to import a few from Africa, to work his farm? Would he

---

* In the first edition of this work, it should read 1816, as above, and not 1826, as it there appears.

work in the hot sun to earn his bread, if he could make an African work for nothing, particularly, if he could keep him in ignorance and make him believe that God made him for nothing
else but to work for him? Is not Mr. Clay a white man, and too
delicate to work in the hot sun! ! Was he not made by his Creator to sit in the shade, and make the blacks work without re-
muneration for their services, to support him and his family! ! !
I have been for some time taking notice of this man's speeches
and public writings, but never to my knowledge have I seen any
thing in his writings which insisted on the emancipation of
slavery, which has almost ruined his country. Thus we see the
depravity of men's hearts, when in pursuit only of gain—particularly when they oppress their fellow creatures to obtain that
gain—God suffers some to go on until they are lost forever. This
same Mr. Clay, wants to know, what he has done, to merit the
disapprobation of the American people. In a public speech delivered by him, he asked: "Did I involve my country in an un-
necessary war?" to merit the censure of the Americans—"Did I
bring obliquy upon the nation, or the people whom I represented?
—did I ever lose any opportunity to advance the fame, honor
and prosperity of this State and the Union?" How astonishing
it is, for a man who knows so much about God and his ways, as
Mr. Clay, to ask such frivolous questions? Does he believe that
a man of his talents and standing in the midst of a people, will
get along unnoticed by the penetrating and all seeing eye of
God, who is continually taking cognizance of the hearts of men?
Is not God against him, for advocating the murderous cause of
slavery? If God is against him, what can the Americans, together with the whole world do for him? Can they save him from
the hand of the Lord Jesus Christ?

I shall now pass in review the speech of Mr. Elias B. Caldwell,
Esq. of the District of Columbia, extracted from the same page
on which Mr. Clay's will be found. Mr. Caldwell, giving his
opinion respecting us, at that ever memorable meeting, he says:
"The more you improve the condition of these people, the more
you cultivate their minds, the more miserable you make them in
their present state. You give them a higher relish for those
privileges which they can never attain, and turn what we intend
for a blessing into a curse." Let me ask this benevolent man,

what he means by a blessing intended for us? Did he mean sinking us and our children into ignorance and wretchedness, to support him and his family? What he meant will appear evident and obvious to the most ignorant in the world ☞ See Mr. Caldwell's intended blessings for us, O! my Lord! ! "No," said he, "if they must remain in their present situation, keep them in the *lowest state of degradation and ignorance.* The nearer you bring them to the condition of brutes, the better chance do you give them of possessing their *apathy."* Here I pause to get breath, having labored to extract the above clause of this gentleman's speech, at that colonizing meeting. I presume that everybody knows the meaning of the word *"apathy,"*—if any do not, let him get Sheridan's Dictionary, in which he will find it explained in full. I solicit the attention of the world, to the foregoing part of Mr. Caldwell's speech, that they may see what man will do with his fellow men, when he has them under his feet. To what length will not man go in iniquity when given up to a hard heart, and reprobate mind, in consequence of blood and oppression? The last clause of this speech, which was written in a very artful manner, and which will be taken for the speech of a friend, without close examination and deep penetration, I shall now present. He says, "surely, Americans ought to be the last people on earth, to advocate such slavish doctrines, to cry peace and contentment to those who are deprived of the privileges of civil liberty, they who have so largely partaken of its blessings, who know so well how to estimate its value, ought to be among the foremost to extend it to others." The real sense and meaning of the last part of Mr. Caldwell's speech is, get the free people of colour away to Africa, from among the slaves, where they may at once be blessed and happy, and those who we hold in slavery, will be contented to rest in ignorance and wretchedness, to dig up gold and silver for us and our children. Men have indeed got to be so cunning, these days, that it would take the eye of a Solomon to penetrate and find them out.

☞ ADDITION.—Our dear Redeemer said, "Therefore, whatsoever ye have spoken in darkness, shall be heard in the light; and that which ye have spoken in the ear in closets, shall be proclaimed upon the house tops."

How obviously this declaration of our Lord has been shown

among the Americans of the United States. They have hitherto passed among some nations, who do not know any thing about their internal concerns, for the most enlightened, humane, charitable, and merciful people upon earth, when at the same time they treat us, the (coloured people) secretly more cruel and unmerciful than any other nation upon earth.—It is a fact, that in our Southern and Western States, there are millions who hold us in chains or in slavery, whose greatest object and glory, is centered in keeping us sunk in the most profound ignorance and stupidity, to make us work without remunerations for our services. Many of whom if they catch a coloured person, whom they hold in unjust ignorance, slavery and degradation, to them and their children, with a book in his hand, will beat him nearly to death. I heard a wretch in the state of North Carolina said, that if any man would teach a black person whom he held in slavery, to spell, read or write, he would prosecute him to the very extent of the law.—Said the ignorant wretch,* "a Nigar, ought not to have any more sense than enough to work for his master." May I not ask to fatten the wretch and his family?—These and similar cruelties these *Christians* have been for hundreds of years inflicting on our fathers and us in the dark, God has however, very recently published some of their secret crimes on the house top, that the world may gaze on their Christianity and see of what kind it is composed.—Georgia for instance, God has completely shown to the world, the *Christianity* among its white *inhabitants*. A law has recently passed the Legislature of this *republican* State (Georgia) prohibiting all free or slave persons of colour, from learning to read or write; another law has passed the *republican* House of Delegates, (but not the Senate) in Virginia, to prohibit all persons of colour, (free and slave) from learning to read or write, and even to hinder them from meeting together in order to worship our Maker! ! ! ! ! !—Now I solemnly appeal, to the most skilful historians in the world, and all those who are mostly acquainted with the histories of the Antideluvians and of Sodom and Gomorrah, to show me a

---

* It is a fact, that in all our Slave-holding States (in the countries) there are thousands of the whites, who are almost as ignorant in comparison as horses, the most they know, is to beat the coloured people, which some of them shall have their hearts full of yet.

parallel of barbarity. *Christians! ! Christians! ! !* I dare you to show me a parallel of cruelties in the annals of Heathens or of Devils, with those of Ohio, Virginia and of Georgia—know the world that these things were before done in the dark, or in a corner under a garb of humanity and religion. God has how-ever, taken of the fig-leaf covering, and made them expose them-selves on the house top. I tell you that God works in many ways his wonders to perform, he will unless they repent, make them expose themselves enough more yet to the world.—See the acts of the *Christians* in FLORIDA, SOUTH CAROLINA, and KEN-TUCKY—was it not for the reputation of the house of my Lord and Master, I would mention here, an act of cruelty inflicted a few days since on a black man, by the white *Christians* in the PARK STREET CHURCH, in this (CITY) which is almost enough to make Demons themselves quake and tremble in their FIREY HABITATIONS.—Oh! my Lord how refined in iniquity the whites have got to be in consequence of our blood*—what kind! ! Oh ! what kind! ! ! of Christianity can be found this day in all the earth! ! ! ! !

I write without the fear of man, I am writing for my God, and fear none but himself; they may put me to death if they choose—(I fear and esteem a good man however, let him be black or white.) I forbear to comment on the cruelties inflicted on this Black Man by the Whites, in the Park Street MEETING HOUSE, I will leave it in the dark! ! ! ! ! But I declare that the atrocity is really to Heaven daring and infernal, that I must say that God has commenced a course of exposition among the Americans, and the glorious and heavenly work will continue to progress until they learn to do justice.☜❧

Extract from the Speech of Mr. John Randolph, of Roanoke.

Said he:—"It had been properly observed by the Chairman, as well as by the gentleman from this District (meaning Messrs. Clay and Caldwell) that there was nothing in the proposition submitted to consideration which in the smallest degree touches

---

* The Blood of our fathers who have been murdered by the whites, and the groans of our Brethren, who are now held in cruel ignorance, wretched-ness and slavery by them, cry aloud to the Maker of Heaven and of earth, against the whole continent of America, for redresses. [The Georgia and Vir-ginia actions, together with the Southern reaction generally, are discussed in the Introduction. The allusion to Ohio has to do with an 1829 law restricting the rights of free Negroes. Ed.]

another very important and delicate question, which ought to be left as much out of view as possible, (Negro Slavery.)*

"There is no fear," Mr. R. said, "that this proposition would alarm the slave-holders; they had been accustomed to think seriously of the subject.—There was a popular work on agriculture, by John Taylor of Carolina [Caroline], which was widely circulated, and much confided in, in Virginia. In that book, much read because coming from a practical man, this description of people, [referring to us half free ones] were pointed out as a great evil. They had indeed been held up as the greater bug-bear to every man who feels an inclination to emancipate his slaves, not to create in the bosom of his country so great a nuisance. If a place could be provided for their reception, and a mode of sending them hence, there were hundreds, nay thousands of citizens who would, by manumitting their slaves, relieve themselves from the cares attendant on their possession. The great slave-holder," Mr. R. said, "was frequently a mere sentry at his own door—bound to stay on his plantation to see that his slaves were properly treated, &c." Mr. R. concluded by saying, that he had thought it necessary to make these remarks being a slave-holder himself, to shew that, "so far from being connected with abolition of slavery, the measure proposed would prove one of the greatest securities to enable the master to keep in possession his own property."

Here is a demonstrative proof, of a plan got up, by a gang of slave-holders to select the free people of colour from among the slaves, that our more miserable brethren may be the better secured in ignorance and wretchedness, to work their farms and dig their mines, and thus go on enriching the Christians with their blood and groans. What our brethren could have been thinking about, who have left their native land and home and gone away to Africa, I am unable to say. This country is as much ours as it is the whites, whether they will admit it now or not, they will see and believe it by and by. They tell us about

---

* "Niger," is a word derived from the Latin, which was used by the old Romans, to designate inanimate beings, which were black: such as soot, pot, wood, house, &c. Also, animals which they considered inferior to the human species, as a black horse, cow, hog, bird, dog, &c. The white Americans have applied this term to Africans, by way of reproach for our colour, to aggravate and heighten our miseries, because they have their feet on our throats.

prejudice—what have we to do with it? Their prejudices will be obliged to fall like lightning to the ground, in succeeding generations; not, however, with the will and consent of all the whites, for some will be obliged to hold on to the old adage, viz: the blacks are not men, but were made to be an inheritance to us and our children for ever! ! ! ! ! ! I hope the residue of the coloured people, will stand still and see the salvation of God and the miracle which he will work for our delivery from wretchedness under the Christians! ! ! ! ! !

☞ADDITION.—If any of us see fit to go away, go to those who have been for many years, and are now our greatest earthly friends and benefactors—the English. If not so, go to our brethren, the Haytians, who, according to their word, are bound to protect and comfort us. The Americans say, that we are ungrateful—but I ask them for heaven's sake, what should we be grateful to them for—for murdering our fathers and mothers?—Or do they wish us to return thanks to them for chaining and handcuffing us, branding us, cramming fire down our throats, or for keeping us in slavery, and beating us nearly or quite to death to make us work in ignorance and miseries, to support them and their families. They certainly think that we are a gang of fools. Those among them, who have volunteered their services for our redemption, though we are unable to compensate them for their labours, we nevertheless thank them from the bottom of our hearts, and have our eyes steadfastly fixed upon them, and their labours of love for God and man.—But do slave-holders think that we thank them for keeping us in miseries, and taking our lives by the inches?☜

Before I proceed further with this scheme, I shall give an extract from the letter of that truly Reverend Divine, (Bishop Allen,) of Philadelphia, respecting this trick. At the instance of the editor of the Freedom's Journal, he says, * "Dear Sir, I have

* See Freedom's Journal for Nov. 2d, 1827—vol. 1, No. 34. [Richard Allen, 1760-1831, was born a slave in Philadelphia. He founded the African Methodist Episcopal Church and became its first bishop. *Freedom's Journal,* edited by Samuel E. Cornish and John B. Russwurm, was the first Negro newspaper in the United States. It began publication in New York City on March 16, 1827, continuing into 1829, when Russwurm "defected" to the Colonization Society and emigrated to Liberia. Walker was Boston agent for *Freedom's Journal* and an occasional contributor to it. Ed.]

been for several years trying to reconcile my mind to the Colonizing of Africans in Liberia, but there have always been, and there
still remain great and insurmountable objections against the
scheme. We are an unlettered people, brought up in ignorance,
not one in a hundred can read or write, not one in a thousand
has a liberal education; is there any fitness for such to be sent
into a far country, among heathens, to convert or civilize them,
when they themselves are neither civilized or Christianized? See
the great bulk of the poor, ignorant Africans in this country,
exposed to every temptation before them: all for the want of their
morals being refined by education and proper attendance paid
unto them by their owners, or those who had the charge of them.
It is said by the Southern slave-holders, that the more ignorant
they can bring up the Africans, the better slaves they make, ('go
and come.') Is there any fitness for such people to be colonized
in a far country to be their own rulers? Can we not discern
the project of sending the free people of colour away from their
country? Is it not for the interest of the slave-holders to select
the free people of colour out of the different states, and send
them to Liberia? Will it not make their slaves uneasy to see free
men of colour enjoying liberty? It is against the law in some
of the Southern States, that a person of colour should receive
an education, under a severe penalty. Colonizationists speak of
America being first colonized; but is there any comparison between the two? America was colonized by as *wise, judicious* and
educated men as the world afforded. WILLIAM PENN did not
want for *learning, wisdom,* or *intelligence.* If all the people in
Europe and America were as ignorant and in the same situation
as our brethren, what would become of the world? Where would
be the principle or piety that would govern the people? We were
stolen from our mother country, and brought *here.* We have
tilled the ground and made fortunes for thousands, and still they
are not weary of our services. *But they who stay to till the
ground must be slaves.* Is there not land enough in America, or
'corn enough in Egypt?' Why should they send us into a far
country to die? See the thousands of foreigners emigrating to
America every year: and if there be ground sufficient for them to
cultivate, and bread for them to eat, why would they wish to
send the *first tillers* of the land away? Africans have made for-

tunes for thousands, who are yet unwilling to part with their
services; but the free must be sent away, and those who remain,
must be *slaves*. I have no doubt that there are many good men
who do not see as I do, and who are for sending us to Liberia;
but they have not duly considered the subject—they are not men
of colour.—This land which we have watered with our *tears*
and *our blood*, is now our *mother country*, and we are well satisfied to stay where wisdom abounds and the gospel is free."

"RICHARD ALLEN,
"*Bishop of the African Methodist Episcopal*
"*Church in the United States.*"

I have given you, my brethren, an extract verbatim, from the
letter of that godly man, as you may find it on the aforemen-
tioned page of Freedom's Journal. I know that thousands, and
perhaps millions of my brethren in these States, have never heard
of such a man as Bishop Allen—a man whom God many years ago
raised up among his ignorant and degraded brethren, to preach
Jesus Christ and him crucified to them—who notwithstanding,
had to wrestle against principalities and the powers of darkness
to diffuse that gospel with which he was endowed among his
brethren—but who having overcome the combined powers of
devils and wicked men, has under God planted a Church among
us which will be as durable as the foundation of the earth on
which it stands. Richard Allen! O my God! ! The bare recol-
lection of the labours of this man, and his ministers among his
deplorably wretched brethren, (rendered so by the whites) to
bring them to a knowledge of the God of Heaven, fills my soul
with all those very high emotions which would take the pen of
an Addison to portray. It is impossible my brethren for me to
say much in this work respecting that man of God. When the
Lord shall raise up coloured historians in succeeding generations,
to present the crimes of this nation, to the then gazing world,
the Holy Ghost will make them do justice to the name of Bishop
Allen, of Philadelphia. Suffice it for me to say, that the name
of this very man (Richard Allen) though now in obscurity and
degradation, will notwithstanding, stand on the pages of history
among the greatest divines who have lived since the apostolic

age, and among the Africans, Bishop Allen's will be entirely preeminent. My brethren, search after the character and exploits
of this godly man among his ignorant and miserable brethren, to
bring them to a knowledge of the truth as it is in our Master.
Consider upon the tyrants and false Christians against whom
he had to contend in order to get access to his brethren. See him
and his ministers in the States of New York, New Jersey, Penn-
sylvania, Delaware and Maryland, carrying the gladsome tidings
of free and full salvation to the coloured people. Tyrants and
false Christians however, would not allow him to penetrate far
into the South, for fear that he would awaken some of his ignorant brethren, whom they held in wretchedness and misery—
for fear, I say it, that he would awaken and bring them to a
knowledge of their Maker. O my Master! my Master! I cannot but think upon Christian Americans! ! !—What kind of people can they be? Will not those who were burnt up in Sodom and
Gomorrah rise up in judgment against Christian Americans with
the Bible in their hands, and condemn them? Will not the Scribes
and Pharisees of Jerusalem, who had nothing but the laws of
Moses and the Prophets to go by, rise up in judgment against
Christian Americans, and condemn them,* who, in addition to
these have a revelation from Jesus Christ the Son of the living
God? In fine, will not the Antideluvians, together with the whole
heathen world of antiquity, rise up in judgment against Christian Americans and condemn them? The Christians of Europe
and America go to Africa, bring us away, and throw us into
the seas, and in other ways murder us, as they would wild beast.
The Antideluvians and heathens never dreamed of such barbari-
ties.—Now the Christians believe, because they have a name to
live, while they are dead, that God will overlook such things.
But if he does not deceive them, it will be because he has over-
looked it sure enough. But to return to this godly man, Bishop
Allen. I do hereby openly affirm it to the world, that he has
done more in a spiritual sense for his ignorant and wretched
brethren than any other man of colour has, since the world began.
And as for the greater part of the whites, it has hitherto been

---

* I mean those whose labours for the good, or rather destruction of Jerusalem,
and the Jews ceased before our Lord entered the Temple, and overturned the
tables of the Money Changers.

their greatest object and glory to keep us ignorant of our Maker, so as to make us believe that we were made to be slaves to them and their children, to dig up gold and silver for them. It is notorious that not a few professing Christians among the whites, who profess to love our Lord and Saviour Jesus Christ, have assailed this man and laid all the obstacles in his way they possibly could, consistent with their profession—and what for? Why, their course of proceeding and his, clashed exactly together —they trying their best to keep us ignorant, that we might be the better and more obedient slaves—while he, on the other hand, doing his very best to enlighten us and teach us a knowledge of the Lord. And I am sorry that I have it to say, that many of our brethren have joined in with our oppressors, whose dearest objects are only to keep us ignorant and miserable against this man to stay his hand.—However, they have kept us in so much ignorance, that many of us know no better than to fight against ourselves, and by that means strengthen the hands of our natural enemies, to rivet their infernal chains of slavery upon us and our children. I have several times called the white Americans our *natural enemies*—I shall here define my meaning of the phrase. Shem, Ham and Japheth, together with their father Noah and wives, I believe were not 'natural enemies to each other. When the ark rested after the flood upon Mount Arrarat, in Asia, they (eight) were all the people which could be found alive in all the earth—in fact if Scriptures be true, (which I believe are) there were no other living men in all the earth, notwithstanding some ignorant creatures hesitate not to tell us that we, (the blacks) are the seed of Cain the murderer of his brother Abel. But where or of whom those ignorant and avaricious wretches could have got their information, I am unable to declare. Did they receive it from the Bible? I have searched the Bible as well as they, if I am not as well learned as they are, and have never seen a verse which testifies whether we are the seed of Cain or of Abel. Yet those men tell us that we are the seed of Cain, and that God put a dark stain upon us, that we might be known as their slaves! ! ! Now, I ask those avaricious and ignorant wretches, who act more like the seed of Cain, by murdering the whites or the blacks? How many vessel loads of human beings,

have the blacks thrown into the seas? How many thousand souls
have the blacks murdered in cold blood, to make them work in
wretchedness and ignorance, to support them and their families? *
—However, let us be the seed of *Cain, Harry, Dick,* or *Tom! ! !*
God will show the whites what we are, yet. I say, from the beginning, I do not think that we were natural enemies to each other.
But the whites having made us so wretched, by subjecting us to
slavery, and having murdered so many millions of us, in order
to make us work for them, and out of devilishness—and they
taking our wives, whom we love as we do ourselves—our mothers,
who bore the pains of death to give us birth—our fathers and
dear little children, and ourselves, and strip and beat us one
before the other—chain, hand-cuff, and drag us about like rattle-
snakes—shoot us down like wild bears, before each other's faces,
to make us submissive to, and work to support them and their
families. They (the whites) know well, if we are *men*—and
there is a secret monitor in their hearts which tells them we are
—they know, I say, if we *are* men, and see them treating us in
the manner they do, that there can be nothing in our hearts but
death alone, for them, notwithstanding we may appear cheerful,
when we see them murdering our dear mothers and wives, because
we cannot help ourselves. Man, in all ages and all nations of
the earth, is the same. Man is a peculiar creature—he is the
image of his God, though he may be subjected to the most
wretched condition upon earth, yet the spirit and feeling which
constitute the creature, man, can never be entirely erased from
his breast, because the God who made him after his own image,
planted it in his heart; he cannot get rid of it. The whites
knowing this, they do not know what to do; they know that they
have done us so much injury, they are afraid that we, being men,
and not brutes, will retaliate, and woe will be to them; therefore, that dreadful fear, together with an avaricious spirit, and
the natural love in them, to be called masters, (which term will
yet honour them with to their sorrow) bring them to the resolve

* How many millions souls of the human family have the blacks beat nearly
to death, to keep them from learning to read the Word of God, and from
writing. And telling lies about them, by holding them up to the world as a
tribe of TALKING APES, void of INTELLECT!!!!! *incapable* of LEARN-
ING, &c.

that they will keep us in ignorance and wretchedness, as long as they possibly can,* and make the best of their time, while it lasts. Consequently they, themselves, (and not us) render themselves our natural enemies, by treating us so cruel. They keep us miserable now, and call us their property, but some of them will have enough of us by and by—their stomachs shall run over with us; they want us for their slaves, and shall have us to their fill. We are all in the world together! !—I said above, because we cannot help ourselves, (viz. we cannot help the whites murdering our mothers and our wives) but this statement is incorrect —for we can help ourselves; for, if we lay aside abject servility, and be determined to act like men, and not brutes—the murderers among the whites would be afraid to show their cruel heads. But O, my God!—in sorrow I must say it, that my colour, all over the world, have a mean, servile spirit. They yield in a moment to the whites, let them be right or wrong—the reason they are able to keep their feet on our throats. Oh! my coloured brethren, all over the world, when shall we arise from this death-like apathy?—And be men! ! You will notice, if ever we become men, (I mean *respectable* men, such as other people are,) we must exert ourselves to the full. For remember, that it is the greatest desire and object of the greater part of the whites, to keep us ignorant, and make us work to support them and their families.— Here now, in the Southern and Western sections of this country, there are at least three coloured persons for one white, why is it, that those few weak, good-for-nothing whites, are able to keep so many able men, one of whom, can put to flight a dozen whites, in wretchedness and misery? It shows at once, what the blacks are, we are ignorant, abject, servile and mean—and the whites

* And still holds us up with indignity as being incapable of acquiring knowledge!!! See the inconsistency of the assertions of those wretches—they beat us inhumanely, sometimes almost to death, for attempting to inform ourselves, by reading the *Word* of our Maker, and at the same time tell us, that we are beings *void of intellect!!!!* How admirably their practices agree with their professions in this case. Let me cry shame upon you Americans, for such outrages upon human nature!!! If it were possible for the whites always to keep us ignorant and miserable, and make us work to enrich them and their children, and insult our feelings by representing us as *talking Apes*, what would they do? But glory, honour and praise to Heaven's King, that the sons and daughters of Africa, will, in spite of all the opposition of their enemies, stand forth in all the dignity and glory that is granted by the Lord to his creature man.

know it—they know that we are too servile to assert our rights as men—or they would not fool with us as they do. Would they fool with any other peoples as they do with us? No, they know too well, that they would get themselves ruined. Why do they not bring the inhabitants of Asia to be body servants to them? They know they would get their bodies rent and torn from head to foot. Why do they not get the Aborigines of this country to be slaves to them and their children, to work their farms and dig their mines? They know well that the Aborigines of this country, or (Indians) would tear them from the earth. The Indians would not rest day or night, they would be up all times of night, cut‧ting their cruel throats. But my colour, (some, not all,) are willing to stand still and be murdered by the cruel whites. In some of the West-Indies Islands, and over a large part of South America, there are six or eight coloured persons for one white.*

* For instance in the two States of Georgia, and South Carolina, there are, perhaps, not much short of six or seven hundred thousand persons of colour; and if I was a gambling character, I would not be afraid to stake down upon the board FIVE CENTS against TEN, that there are in the single State of Virginia, five or six hundred thousand Coloured persons. Four hundred and fifty thousand of whom (let them be well equipt for war) I would put against every white person on the whole continent of America. (Why? why because I know that the Blacks, once they get involved in a war, had rather die than to live, they either kill or be killed.) The whites know this too, which make them quake and tremble. To show the world further, how servile the coloured people are, I will only hold up to view, the one Island of Jamaica, as a speci-men of our meanness.

In that Island, there are three hundred and fifty thousand souls—of whom fifteen thousand are whites, the remainder, three hundred and thirty-five thousand are coloured people! and this Island is ruled by the white people!!! !!!!! (15,000) ruling and tyranizing over 335,000 persons!!!!!!!!—O! coloured men!! O! coloured men!!! O! coloured men!!!! Look!! look!!! at this!!!! and, tell me if we are not abject and servile enough, how long, O! how long my colour shall we be dupes and dogs to the cruel whites?—I only passed Jamaica, and its inhabitants, in review as a specimen to show the world, the condition of the Blacks at this time, now coloured people of the whole world, I beg you to look at the (15000 white,) and (Three Hundred and Thirty-five Thousand coloured people) in that Island, and tell me how can the white tyrants of the world but say that we are not men, but were made to be slaves and Dogs to them and their children forever!!!!!!!—why my friend only look at the thing!!!! (15000) whites keeping in wretchedness and degra-dation (335000) viz. 22 coloured persons for one white !!!!!!! when at the same time, an equal number (15000) Blacks, would almost take the whole of South America, because where they go as soldiers to fight death follows in their train.

Why do they not take possession of those places? Who hinders them? It is not the avaricious whites—for they are too busily engaged in laying up money—derived from the blood and tears of the blacks. The fact is, they are too servile, they love to have Masters too well! ! Some of our brethren, too, who seeking more after self aggrandisement, than the glory of God, and the welfare of their brethren, join in with our oppressors, to ridicule and say all manner of evils falsely against our Bishop. They think, that they are doing great things, when they can get in company with the whites, to ridicule and make sport of those who are labouring for their good. Poor ignorant creatures, they do not know that the sole aim and object of the whites, are only to make fools and slaves of them, and put the whip to them, and make them work to support them and their families. But I do say, that no man, can well be a despiser of Bishop Allen, for his public labours among us, unless he is a despiser of God and of Righteousness. Thus, we see, my brethren, the two very opposite positions of those great men, who have written respecting this "Colonizing Plan." (Mr. Clay and his slave-holding party,) men who are resolved to keep us in eternal wretchedness, are also bent upon sending us to Liberia. While the Reverend Bishop Allen, and his party, men who have the fear of God, and the wellfare of their brethren at heart. The Bishop, in particular, whose labours for the salvation of his brethren, are well known to a large part of those, who dwell in the United States, are completely opposed to the plan—and advise us to stay where we are. Now we have to determine whose advice we will take respecting this all important matter, whether we will adhere to Mr. Clay and his slave holding party, who have always been our oppressors and murderers, and who are for colonizing us, more through apprehension than humanity, or to this godly man who has done so much for our benefit, together with the advice of all the good and wise among us and the whites. Will any of us leave our homes and go to Africa? I hope not.* Let them commence their attack upon us as they did on our brethren in Ohio,

---

* Those who are ignorant enough to go to Africa, the coloured people ought to be glad to have them go, for if they are ignorant enough to let the whites *fool* them off to Africa, they would be no small injury to us if they reside in this country.

driving and beating us from our country, and my soul for theirs, they will have enough of it. Let no man of us budge one step, and let slave-holders come to beat us from our country. America is more our country, than it is the whites—we have enriched it with our *blood and tears*. The greatest riches in all America have arisen from our blood and tears:—and will they drive us from our property and homes, which we have earned with our *blood?* They must look sharp or this very thing will bring swift destruction upon them. The Americans have got so fat on our blood and groans, that they have almost forgotten the God of armies. But let them go on.

☞ADDITION.—I will give here a very imperfect list of the cruelties inflicted on us by the enlightened Christians of America. —First, no trifling portion of them will beat us nearly to death, if they find us on our knees praying to God,—They hinder us from going to hear the word of God—they keep us sunk in ignorance, and will not let us learn to read the word of God, nor write—If they find us with a book of any description in our hand, they will beat us nearly to death—they are so afraid we will learn to read, and enlighten our dark and benighted minds—They will not suffer us to meet together to worship the God who made us— they brand us with hot iron—they cram bolts of fire down our throats—they cut us as they do horses, bulls, or hogs—they crop our ears and sometimes cut off bits of our tongues—they chain and hand-cuff us, and while in that miserable and wretched condition, beat us with cow-hides and clubs—they keep us half naked and starve us sometimes nearly to death under their infernal whips or lashes (which some of them shall have enough of yet)—They put on us fifty-sixes and chains, and make us work in that cruel situation, and in sickness, under lashes to support them and their families.—They keep us three or four hundred feet under ground working in their mines, night and day to dig up gold and silver to enrich them and their children.—They keep us in the most death-like ignorance by keeping us from all source of information, and call us, who are free men and next to the Angels of God, their property! ! ! ! ! ! They make us fight and murder each other, many of us being ignorant, not knowing any better.—They take us, (being ignorant,) and put us as drivers one over the other, and make us afflict each other as bad as they

themselves afflict us—and to crown the whole of this catalogue of
cruelties, they tell us that we the (blacks) are an inferior race of
beings! incapable of self government! !—We would be injurious to society and ourselves, if tyrants should loose their unjust
hold on us! ! ! That if we were free we would not work, but
would live on plunder or theft! ! ! ! that we are the meanest
and laziest set of beings in the world! ! ! ! ! That they are
obliged to keep us in bondage to do us good! ! ! ! ! !—That
we are satisfied to rest in slavery to them and their children! !
! ! ! !—That we ought not to be set free in America, but ought
to be sent away to Africa! ! ! ! ! ! ! !—That if we were set
free in America, we would involve the country in a civil war,
which assertion is altogether at variance with our feeling or
design, for we ask them for nothing but the rights of man, viz.
for them to set us free, and treat us like men, and there will be
no danger, for we will love and respect them, and protect our
country—but cannot conscientiously do these things until they
treat us like men.

How cunning slave-holders think they are! ! !—How much
like the king of Egypt who, after he saw plainly that God was
determined to bring out his people, in spite of him and his, as
powerful as they were. He was willing that Moses, Aaron and
the Elders of Israel, but not all the people should go and serve
the Lord. But God deceived him as he will Christian Americans,
unless they are very cautious how they move. What would have
become of the United States of America, was it not for those
among the whites, who not in words barely, but in truth and in
deed, love and fear the Lord?—Our Lord and Master said:—*
"[But] Whoso shall offend one of these little ones which believe
in me, it were better for him that a millstone were hanged about
his neck, and that he were drowned in the depth of the sea."
But the Americans with this very threatening of the Lord's, not
only beat his little ones among the Africans, but many of them
they put to death or murder. Now the avaricious Americans,
think that the Lord Jesus Christ will let them off, because his
words are no more than the words of a man! ! ! In fact, many
of them are so avaricious and ignorant, that they do not believe
in our Lord and Saviour Jesus Christ. Tyrants may think they

* See St. Matthew's Gospel, chap. xviii. 6.

are so skillful in State affairs is the reason that the government is preserved. But I tell you, that this country would have been given up long ago, was it not for the lovers of the Lord. They are indeed, the salt of the earth. Remove the people of God among the whites, from this land of blood, and it will stand until they cleverly get out of the way.

I adopt the language of the Rev. Mr. S. E. Cornish, of New York, editor of the Rights of All,* and say: "Any coloured man of common intelligence, who gives his countenance and influence to that colony, further than its missionary object and interest extend, should be considered as a traitor to his brethren, and discarded by every respectable man of colour. And every member of that society, however pure his motive, whatever may be his religious character and moral worth, should in his efforts to remove the coloured population from their rightful soil, the land of their birth and nativity, be considered as acting gratuitously unrighteous and cruel."

Let me make an appeal brethren, to your hearts, for your cordial co-operation in the circulation of "The Rights of All," among us. The utility of such a vehicle conducted, cannot be estimated. I hope that the well informed among us, may see the absolute necessity of their co-operation in its universal spread among us. If we should let it go down, never let us undertake any thing of the kind again, but give up at once and say that we are really so ignorant and wretched that we cannot do any thing at all! !—As far as I have seen the writings of its editor, I believe he is not seeking to fill his pockets with money, but has the welfare of his brethren truly at heart. Such men, brethren, ought to be supported by us.

But to return to the colonizing trick. It will be well for me to notice here at once, that I do not mean indiscriminately to condemn all the members and advocates of this scheme, for I believe that there are some friends to the sons of Africa, who are laboring for our salvation, not in words only but in truth and in deed, who have been drawn into this plan—Some, more by persuasion than any thing else; while others, with humane feelings and lively zeal for our good, seeing how much we suffer from

* [*Rights of All,* first appearing in May, 1829, was successor to *Freedom's Journal. Cf.* editor's note on page 56. Ed.]

the afflictions poured upon us by unmerciful tyrants, are willing
to enroll their names in any thing which they think has for its
ultimate end our redemption from wretchedness and miseries;
such men, with a heart truly overflowing with gratitude for their
past services and zeal in our cause, I humbly beg to examine
this plot minutely, and see if the end which they have in view
will be completely consummated by such a course of procedure.
Our friends who have been imperceptibly drawn into this plot I
view with tenderness, and would not for the world injure their
feelings, and I have only to hope for the future, that they will
withdraw themselves from it;—for I declare to them, that the
plot is not for the glory of God, but on the contrary the perpetua-
tion of slavery in this country, which will ruin them and the
country forever, unless something is immediately done.

Do the colonizationists think to send us off without first being
reconciled to us? Do they think to bundle us up like brutes and
send us off, as they did our brethren of the State of Ohio? *
Have they not to be reconciled to us, or reconcile us to them,
for the cruelties with which they have afflicted our fathers and
us? Methinks colonizationists think they have a set of brutes
to deal with, sure enough. Do they think to drive us from our
country and homes, after having enriched it with our blood and
tears, and keep back millions of our dear brethren, sunk in the
most barbarous wretchedness, to dig up gold and silver for them
and their children? Surely, the Americans must think that we are
brutes, as some of them have represented us to be. They think
that we do not feel for our brethren, whom they are murdering
by the inches, but they are dreadfully deceived. I acknowledge
that there are some deceitful and hypocritical wretches among
us, who will tell us one thing while they mean another, and
thus they go on aiding our enemies to oppress themselves and
us. But I declare this day before my Lord and Master, that I

* The great slave holder, Mr. John Randolph, of Virginia, intimated in one
of his *great, happy* and *eloquent* HARRANGUES, before the Virginia Convention,
that Ohio is a slave State, by ranking it among other Slave-holding States.
This probably was done by the HONORABLE *Slave-holder* to deter the minds of
the ignorant; to such I would say, that Ohio always was and is now a free
State, that it never was and I do not believe it ever will be a slave-holding
State; the people I believe, though some of them are hard hearted enough,
detest Slavery too much to admit an evil into their bosom, which gnaws into
the very vitals, and sinews of those who are now in possession of it.

believe there are some true-hearted sons of Africa, in this land of oppression, but pretended *liberty! ! ! !*—who do in reality feel for their suffering brethren, who are held in bondage by tyrants. Some of the advocates of this cunningly devised plot of Satan represent us to be the greatest set of cut-throats in the world, as though God wants us to take his work out of his hand before he is ready. Does not vengeance belong to the Lord? Is he not able to repay the Americans for their cruelties, with which they have afflicted Africa's sons and daughters, without our interference, unless we are ordered? It is surprising to think that the Americans, having the Bible in their hands, do not believe it. Are not the hearts of all men in the hands of the God of battles? And does he not suffer some, in consequence of cruelties, to go on until they are irrecoverably lost? Now, what can be more aggravating, than for the Americans, after having treated us so bad, to hold us up to the world as such great throat-cutters? It appears to me as though they are resolved to assail us with every species of affliction that their ingenuity can invent. ☞ See the African Repository and Colonial Journal, from its commencement to the present day—see how we are through the medium of that periodical, abused and held up by the Americans, as the greatest nuisance to society, and throat-cutters in the world.) But the Lord sees their actions. Americans! notwithstanding you have and do continue to treat us more cruel than any heathen nation ever did a people it had subjected to the same condition that you have us. Now let us reason—I mean you of the United States, whom I believe God designs to save from destruction, if you will hear. For I declare to you, whether you believe it or not, that there are some on the continent of America, who will never be able to repent. God will surely destroy them, to show you his disapprobation of the murders they and you have inflicted on us. I say, let us reason; had you not better take our body, while you have it in your power, and while we are yet ignorant and wretched, not knowing but a little, give us education, and teach us the pure religion of our Lord and Master, which is calculated to make the lion lay down in peace with the lamb, and which millions of you have beaten us nearly to death for trying to obtain since we have been among you, and thus at once, gain our affection while we are ignorant? Remember Americans, that we must and shall be free and enlightened as you are, will you wait until we shall, under God, obtain our liberty by the crushing arm of power? Will it not be dreadful for you? I speak Americans for your good. We must and shall be free I say, in spite of you. You may do your best to keep us in wretchedness and misery, to enrich you and your children; but God will deliver us from under you. And wo, wo, will be to you if we have to obtain our freedom by fighting. Throw away your fears and prejudices then, and enlighten us and treat us like men, and we will like you more than we do now hate you,* and tell us now no more about colonization, for America is as much our country, as it is yours.—Treat us like men, and there is no danger but we will all live in peace and happiness together. For we are not like you, hard hearted, unmerciful, and unforgiving. What a happy country this will be, if the whites will listen. What nation under heaven, will be able to do any thing with us, unless God gives us up into its hand? But Americans, I declare to you, while you keep us and our children in bondage, and treat us like brutes, to make us support you and your families, we cannot be your friends. You do not look for it, do you? Treat us then like men, and we will be your friends. And there is not a doubt in my mind, but that the whole of the past will be sunk into oblivion, and we yet, under God, will become a united and happy people. The whites may say it is impossible, but remember that nothing is impossible with God.

The Americans may say or do as they please, but they have to raise us from the condition of brutes to that of respectable men, and to make a national acknowledgement to us for the wrongs they have inflicted on us. As unexpected, strange, and wild as these propositions may to some appear, it is no less a fact, that unless they are complied with, the Americans of the United States, though they may for a little while escape, God will yet weigh them in a balance, and if they are not superior to other men, as they have represented themselves to be, he will give them wretchedness to their very heart's content.

And now brethren, having concluded these four Articles, I submit them, together with my Preamble, dedicated to the Lord, for

* You are not astonished at my saying we hate you, for if we are men, we cannot but hate you, while you are treating us like dogs.

your inspection, in language so very simple, that the most ignorant, who can read at all, may easily understand—of which
you may make the best you possibly can.* Should tyrants take
it into their heads to emancipate any of you, remember that your
freedom is your natural right. You are men, as well as they, and
instead of returning thanks to them for your freedom, return it
to the Holy Ghost, who is our rightful owner. If they do not want
to part with your labours, which have enriched them, let them
keep you, and my word for it, that God Almighty, will break
their strong band. Do you believe this, my brethren?—See my
Address, delivered before the General Coloured Association of
Massachusetts, which may be found in Freedom's Journal, for
Dec. 20, 1828.—See the last clause of that Address. Whether you
believe it or not, I tell you that God will dash tyrants, in
combination with devils, into atoms, and will bring you out
from your wretchedness and miseries under these *Christian
People! ! ! ! !*

Those philanthropists and lovers of the human family, who
have volunteered their services for our redemption from wretchedness, have a high claim on our gratitude, and we should always
view them as our greatest earthly benefactors.

If any are anxious to ascertain who I am, know the world, that
I am one of the oppressed, degraded and wretched sons of Africa,
rendered so by the avaricious and unmerciful, among the whites.
—If any wish to plunge me into the wretched incapacity of a
slave, or murder me for the truth, know ye, that I am in the hand

---

* Some of my brethren, who are sensible, do not take an interest in enlightening the minds of our more ignorant brethren respecting this Book, and
in reading it to them, just as though they will not have either to stand or fall
by what is written in this book. Do they believe that I would be so foolish
as to put out a book of this kind without strict—ah! very strict command-
ments of the Lord?—Surely the blacks and whites must think that I am
ignorant enough.—Do they think that I would have the audacious wickedness
to take the name of my God in vain?

Notice, I said in the concluding clause of Article 3—I call God, I call Angels,
I call men to witness, that the destruction of the Americans is at hand, and
will be speedily consummated unless they repent. Now I wonder if the world
think that I would take the name of God in this way in vain? What do they
think I take God to be? Do they suppose that I would trifle with that God
who will not have his Holy name taken in vain?—He will show you and the
world, in due time, whether this book is for his glory, or written by me through
envy to the whites, as some have represented.

of God, and at your disposal. I count my life not dear unto me,
but I am ready to be offered at any moment. For what is the
use of living, when in fact I am dead. But remember, Americans,
that as miserable, wretched, degraded and abject as you have
made us in preceding, and in this generation, to support you and
your families, that some of you, (whites) on the continent of
America, will yet curse the day that you ever were born. You
want slaves, and want us for your slaves! ! ! My colour will yet,
root some of you out of the very face of the earth! ! ! ! ! ! You
may doubt it if you please. I know that thousands will doubt—
they think they have us so well secured in wretchedness, to them
and their children, that it is impossible for such things to occur.*

* Why do the Slave-holders or Tyrants of America and their advocates fight
so hard to keep my brethren from receiving and reading my Book of Appeal
to them?—Is it because they treat us so well?—Is it because we are satisfied
to rest in Slavery to them and their children?—Is it because they are treating
us like men, by compensating us all over this free country!! for our labours?
—But why are the Americans so very fearfully terrified respecting my Book?
—Why do they search vessels, &c. when entering the harbours of tyrannical
States, to see if any of my Books can be found, for fear that my brethren
will get them to read. Why, I thought the Americans proclaimed to the world
that they are a happy, enlightened, humane and Christian people, all the inhabitants of the country enjoy equal Rights!! America is the Asylum for the
oppressed of all nations!!!
Now I ask the Americans to see the fearful terror they labor under for fear
that my brethren will get my Book and read it—and tell me if their declaration is true—viz, if the United States of America is a Republican Government?—Is this not the most tyrannical, unmerciful, and cruel government under Heaven—not excepting the Algerines, Turks and Arabs?—I believe if any
candid person would take the trouble to go through the Southern and Western
sections of this country, and could have the heart to see the cruelties inflicted
by these *Christians* on us, he would say, that the Algerines, Turks and Arabs
treat their dogs a thousand times better than we are treated by the *Christians.*
—But perhaps the Americans do their very best to keep my Brethren from
receiving and reading my "Appeal" for fear they will find in it an extract
which I made from their Declaration of Independence, which says, "we hold
these truths to be self-evident, that all men are created equal," &c. &c. &c.—
If the above are not the causes of the alarm among the Americans, respecting
my Book, I do not know what to impute it to, unless they are possessed of
the same spirit with which Demetrius the Silversmith was possessed—however,
that they may judge whether they are of the same avaricious and ungodly
spirit with that man, I will give here an extract from the Acts of the Apostles,
chapter xix,—verses 23, 24, 25, 26, 27.
"And the same time there arose no small stir about that way. For a certain *man* named Demetrius, a silversmith, which made silver shrines for
Diana, brought no small gain unto the craftsmen; whom he called together
with the workmen of like occupation, and said, Sirs, ye know that by this

So did the antideluvians doubt Noah, until the day in which the flood came and swept them away. So did the Sodomites doubt, until Lot had got out of the city, and God rained down fire and brimstone from Heaven upon them, and burnt them up. So did the king of Egypt doubt the very existence of a God; he said, "who is the Lord, that I should let Israel go?" Did he not find to his sorrow, who the Lord was, when he and all his mighty men of war, were smothered to death in the Red Sea? So did the Romans doubt, many of them were really so ignorant, that they thought the whole of mankind were made to be slaves to them; just as many of the Americans think now, of my colour. But they got dreadfully deceived. When men got their eyes opened, they made the murderers scamper. The way in which they cut their tyrannical throats, was not much inferior to the way the Romans or murderers, served them, when they held them in wretchedness and degradation under their feet. So would Christian Americans doubt, if God should send an Angel from Heaven to preach their funeral sermon. The fact is, the Christians having a name to live, while they are dead, think that God will screen them on that ground.

See the hundreds and thousands of us that are thrown into the seas by Christians, and murdered by them in other ways. They cram us into their vessel holds in chains and in hand-cuffs—men, women and children, all together!! O! save us, we pray thee, thou God of Heaven and of earth, from the devouring hands of the white Christians! ! !

> Oh! thou Alpha and Omega!
> The beginning and the end,
> Enthron'd thou art, in Heaven above,
> Surrounded by Angels there.

craft we have our wealth: moreover, ye see and hear, that not alone at Ephesus, but almost throughout all Asia, this Paul hath persuaded and turned away much people, saying, that they be no gods which are made with hands: so that not only this our craft is in danger to be set at nought; but also that the temple of the great goddess Diana should be despised, and her magnificence should be destroyed, whom all Asia and the world worshippeth."

I pray you Americans of North and South America, together with the whole European inhabitants of the world, (I mean Slave-holders and their advocates) to read and ponder over the above verses in your minds, and judge whether or not you are of the infernal spirit with that Heathen Demetrius, the Silversmith: In fine I beg you to read the whole chapter through carefully.

From whence thou seest the miseries
To which we are subject;
The whites have murder'd us, O God!
And kept us ignorant of thee.

Not satisfied with this, my Lord!
They throw us in the seas:
Be pleas'd, we pray, for Jesus' sake,
To save us from their grasp.

We believe that, for thy glory's sake,
Thou wilt deliver us;
But that thou may'st effect these things,
Thy glory must be sought.

In conclusion, I ask the candid and unprejudiced of the whole world, to search the pages of historians diligently, and see if the Antideluvians—the Sodomites—the Egyptians—the Babylonians —the Ninevites—the Carthagenians—the Persians—the Macedonians—the Greeks—the Romans—the Mahometans—the Jews —or devils, ever treated a set of human beings, as the white Christians of America do us, the blacks, or Africans. I also ask the attention of the world of mankind to the declaration of these very American people, of the United States.

A declaration made July 4, 1776.

It says, * "When in the course of human events, it becomes necessary for one people to dissolve the political bands which have connected them with another, and to assume among the Powers of the earth, the separate and equal station to which the laws of nature and of nature's God entitle them. A decent respect for the opinions of mankind requires, that they should declare the causes which impel them to the separation.—We hold these truths to be self evident—that all men are created equal, that they are endowed by their Creator with certain unalienable rights: that among these, are life, liberty, and the pursuit of happiness that, to secure these rights, governments are instituted among men, deriving their just powers from the consent of the governed; that when ever any form of government becomes destructive of these ends, it is the right of the people to alter or to abolish it, and to

* See the Declaration of Independence of the United States.

institute a new government laying its foundation on such principles, and organizing its powers in such form, as to them shall seem most likely to effect their safety and happiness. Prudence, indeed, will dictate, that governments long established should not be changed for light and transient causes; and accordingly all experience hath shewn, that mankind are more disposed to suffer, while evils are sufferable, than to right themselves by abolishing the forms to which they are accustomed. But when a long train of abuses and usurpations, pursuing invariably the same object, evinces a design to reduce them under absolute despotism, it is their right it is their duty to throw off such government, and to provide new guards for their future security." See your Declaration Americans! ! ! Do you understand your own language? Hear your language, proclaimed to the world, July 4th, 1776 —☞ "We hold these truths to be self evident—that ALL MEN ARE CREATED EQUAL! ! that they *are endowed by their Creator with certain unalienable rights;* that among these are life, *liberty,* and the pursuit of happiness! !" Compare your own language above, extracted from your Declaration of Independence, with your cruelties and murders inflicted by your cruel and unmerciful fathers and yourselves on our fathers and on us—men who have never given your fathers or you the least provocation! ! ! ! ! !

Hear your language further! ☞ "But when a long train of abuses and usurpation, pursuing invariably the same object, evinces a design to reduce them under absolute despotism, it is their *right*, it is their *duty*, to throw off such government, and to provide new guards for their future security."

Now, Americans! I ask you candidly, was your sufferings under Great Britain, one hundredth part as cruel and tyranical as you have rendered ours under you? Some of you, no doubt, believe that we will never throw off your murderous government and "provide new guards for our future security." If Satan has made you believe it, will he not deceive you? * Do the whites say, I being a black man, ought to be humble, which I readily

* The Lord has not taught the Americans that we will not some day or other throw off their chains and hand-cuffs, from our hands and feet, and their devilish lashes (which some of them shall have enough of yet) from off our backs.

admit? I ask them, ought they not to be as humble as I? or do
they think that they can measure arms with Jehovah? Will not
the Lord yet humble them? or will not these very coloured people
whom they now treat worse than brutes, yet under God, humble
them low down enough? Some of the whites are ignorant enough
to tell us, that we ought to be submissive to them, that they may
keep their feet on our throats. And if we do not submit to be
beaten to death by them, we are bad creatures and of course
must be damned, &c. If any man wishes to hear this doctrine
openly preached to us by the American preachers, let him go into
the Southern and Western sections of this country—I do not
speak from hear say—what I have written, is what I have seen
and heard myself. No man may think that my book is made up of
conjecture—I have travelled and observed nearly the whole of
those things myself, and what little I did not get by my own
observation, I received from those among the whites and blacks,
in whom the greatest confidence may be placed.

The Americans may be as vigilant as they please, but they
cannot be vigilant enough for the Lord, neither can they hide
themselves, where he will not find and bring them out.

> 1 Thy presence why withdraw'st, Lord?
>   Why hid'st thou now thy face,
> When dismal times of deep distress
>   Call for thy wonted grace?
>
> 2 The wicked, swell'd with lawless pride,
>   Have made the poor their prey;
> O let them fall by those designs
>   Which they for others lay.
>
> 3 For straight they triumph, if success
>   Their thriving crimes attend;
> And sordid wretches, whom God hates,
>   Perversely they commend.
>
> 4 To own a pow'r above themselves
>   Their haughty pride disdains;
> And, therefore, in their stubborn mind
>   No thought of God remains.
>
> 5 Oppressive methods they pursue
>   And all their foes they slight;

Because thy judgments, unobserv'd,
    Are far above their sight.

6 They fondly think their prosp'rous state
    Shall unmolested be;
They think their vain design shall thrive,
    From all misfortune free.

7 Vain and deceitful is their speech,
    With curses fill'd, and lies;
By which the mischief of their heart
    They study to disguise.

8 Near public roads they lie conceal'd
    And all their art employ,
The innocent and poor at once
    To rifle and destroy.

9 Not lions, crouching in their dens,
    Surprise their heedless prey
With greater cunning, or express
    More savage rage than they.

10 Sometimes they act the harmless man,
    And modest looks they wear;
That so deceiv'd the poor may less
    Their sudden onset fear.

PART II.

11 For, God, they think, no notice takes,
    Of their unrighteous deeds;
He never minds the suff'ring poor,
    Nor their oppression heeds.

12 But thou, O Lord, at length arise,
    Stretch forth thy mighty arm,
And, by the greatness of thy pow'r,
    Defend the poor from harm.

13 No longer let the wicked vaunt,
    And, proudly boasting, say
"Tush, God regards not what we do;
    "He never will repay."—*Common Prayer Book.*

━━━━━

1 Shall I for fear of feeble man,
The spirit's course in me restrain?
Or, undismay'd in deed and word,
Be a true witness of my Lord.

2 Aw'd by mortal's frown, shall I
 Conceal the word of God Most High!
 How then before thee shall I dare
 To stand, or how thy anger bear?

3 Shall I, to soothe th' unholy throng,
 Soften the truth, or smooth my tongue,
 To gain earth's gilded toys or, flee
 The cross endur'd, my Lord, by thee?

4 What then is he whose scorn I dread?
 Whose wrath or hate makes me afraid
 A man! an heir of death! a slave
 To sin! a bubble on the wave!

5 Yea, let men rage, since thou will spread
 Thy shadowing wings around my head:
 Since in all pain thy tender love
 Will still my sure refreshment prove.

        Wesleys Collection.

☞It may not be understood, when I say my Third and last Edition, I mean to convey the idea, that there will be no more Books of this Third Edition printed, but to notify that there will be no more addition in the body of this Work, or additional Notes to this "Appeal."☜

    THE END

APPENDIX I

This is the text of Walker's speech to the Massachusetts General Colored Association, as printed in Freedom's Journal, *December 19, 1828. Minor editorial alterations are in brackets.*

ADDRESS, *Delivered before the General Colored Association at Boston, by David Walker*

Mr. President,—I cannot but congratulate you, together with my brethren on this highly interesting occasion, the first semi-annual meeting of this Society. When I reflect upon the many impediments through which we have had to conduct its affairs, and see, with emotions of delight, the present degree of eminency to which it has arisen, I cannot, sir, but be of the opinion, that an invisible arm must have been stretched out on our behalf. From the very second conference, which was by us convened, to agitate the proposition respecting this society, to its final consolidatibn, we were by some, opposed, with an avidity and zeal, which, had it been on the opposite side, would have done great honor to themselves. And, sir, but for the undeviating, and truly patriotic exertions of those who were favorable to the formation of this institution, it might have been this day, in a yet unorganized condition. Did I say in an unorganized condition? Yea, had our opponents their way, the very notion of such an institution might have been obliterated from our minds. How strange it is, to see men of sound sense, and of tolerably good judgment, act so diametrically in opposition to their interest; but I forbear making any further comments on this subject, and return to that for which we are convened.

First, then, Mr. President, it is necessary to remark here, at once, that the primary object of this institution, is, to unite the colored population, so far, through the United States of America, as may be practicable and expedient; forming societies, opening, extending, and keeping up correspondences, and not withholding any thing which may have the least tendency to meliorate *our* miserable condition—with the restrictions, however, of not infringing on the articles of its constitution, or that of the United States of America. Now, that we are disunited, is a fact, that no one of common sense will deny; and, that the cause of which, is a powerful auxiliary in keeping us from rising to the scale of reasonable and thinking beings, none but those who delight in our degradation will attempt to contradict. Did I say those who delight in our degradation? Yea, sir, glory in keeping us ignorant and miserable, that we might be the better and the longer slaves. I was credibly informed by a gentleman of unquestionable veracity, that a slaveholder upon finding one of his young slaves with a small spelling book in his hand (not opened) fell upon and beat him almost to death, exclaiming, at the same time, to the child, you will acquire better learning than I or any of my family.

I appeal to every candid and unprejudiced mind, do not all such men glory in our miseries and degradations; and are there not millions whose chief glory centers in this horrid wickedness? Now, Mr. President, those are the very humane, philanthropic, and charitable men who proclaim to the world, that the blacks are such a poor, ignorant and degraded species of beings, that, were they set at liberty, they would die for the want of something to subsist upon, and in consequence of which, they are compelled to keep them in bondage, to do them good.

O Heaven! what will not avarice and the love of despotic sway cause men to do with their fellow creatures, when actually in their power? But, to return whence digressed; it has been asked, in what way will the *General Colored Association* (or the Institution) unite the colored population, so far, in the United States as may be practicable and expedient? to which enquiry I answer, by asking the following: Do not two hundred and eighty years [of] very intolerable sufferings teach us the actual necessity of a general among us? do we not know indeed, the horrid dilemma into which we are, and from which, we must exert ourselves, to be extricated? Shall we keep slumbering on, with our arms completely folded up, exclaiming every now and then, against our miseries, yet never do the least thing to ameliorate our condition, or that of posterity? Shall we not, by such inactivity, leave, or [farther] entail a hereditary degradation on our children, but a little, if at all, inferior to that which our fathers, under all their comparative disadvantages and privations, left on us? In fine, shall we, while almost every other people under Heaven, are making such mighty efforts to better their condition, go around from house to house, enquiring what good associations and societies are going to do for us? Ought we not to form ourselves into a general body, to protect, aid, and assist each other to the utmost of our power, with the beforementioned restrictions?

Yes, Mr. President, it is indispensably our duty to try every scheme that we think will have a tendency to facilitate our salvation, and leave the final result to that God, who holds the destinies of people in the hollow of his hand, and who ever has, and will, repay every nation according to its works.

Will any be so hardy as to say, or even to imagine, that we are incapable of effecting any object which may have a tendency to hasten our emancipation, in consequence of the prevalence of ignorance and poverty among us? That the major part of us are ignorant and poor, I am at this time unprepared to deny.—But shall this deter us from all lawful attempts to bring about the desired object? nay, sir, it should rouse us to greater exertions; there ought to be a spirit of emulation and inquiry among us, a hungering and thirsting after religion; these are requisitions, which, if we ever be so happy as to acquire, will fit us for all the departments of life; and, in my humble opinion, ultimately result in rescuing us from an oppression, unparalleled, I had almost said, in the annals of the world.

But some may even think that our white breathren and friends are making such mighty efforts, for the amelioration of our condition, that we may stand as neutral spectators of the work. That we have very good friends yea, very good, among that body, perhaps none but a few of those who have, ever read at all will deny; and that many of them have gone, and will go, all lengths for our good, is evident, from the very works of the great, the good, and the godlike Granville Sharpe [sic], Wilberforce, Lundy, and the truly patriotic and lamented Mr. Ashmun, late Colonial Agent of Liberia, who, with a zeal which was only equalled by the goodness of his

heart has lost his life in our cause, and a host of others too numerous
to mention: a number of private gentlemen too, who, though they
say but little, are nevertheless engaged for good.* Now, all of those
great, and indeed, good friends whom God has given us I do humbly,
and very gratefully acknowledge. But, that we should co-operate
with them, as far as we are able by uniting and cultivating a spirit
of friendship and of love among us, is obvious, from the very ex-
hibition of our miseries, under which we groan.

Two millions and a half of colored people in these United States,
more than five hundred thousand of whom are about two thirds of
the way free. Now, I ask, if no more than these last were united
(which they must be, or always live as enemies) and resolved to aid
and assist each other to the utmost of their power, what mighty
deeds could be done by them for the good of our cause?

But, Mr. President, instead of a general compliance with these
requisitions, which have a natural tendency to raise us in the esti-
mation of the world, we see, to our sorrow, in the very midst of us,
a gang of villains, who, for the paltry sum of fifty or a hundred
dollars, will kidnap and sell into perpetual slavery their fellow creatures! and, too, of one of their fellow sufferers, whose miseries are
a little more enhanced by the scourges of a tyrant, would abscond
from his pretended owner, to take a little recreation, and unfortu-
nately fall in their way, he is gone! Brethren and fellow sufferers,
I ask you, in the name of God, and of Jesus Christ, shall we suffer
such notorious villains to rest peaceably among us? will they not
take our wives and little ones, more particularly our *little ones,*
when a convenient opportunity will admit and sell them for money
to slave holders, who will doom them to *chains, handcuffs,* and
even unto death? May God open our eyes on these children of the
devil and enemies of all good!

But, sir, this wickedness is scarcely more infernal than that which
was attempted a few months since, against the government of our
brethren, the Haytians, by a consummate rogue, who ought to have,
long since, been *haltered,* but who, I was recently informed, is

---

* [Granville Sharp, 1735–1813, and William Wilberforce, 1759–1833, were leading
British abolitionists. On Lundy, see the Introduction. Jehudi Ashmun, 1794–1828,
was a Congregational missionary who served as the chief agent for the American
Colonization Society in Liberia from 1822 to 1828, when he returned to the United
States broken down by disease. Ed.]

nevertheless, received into company among some of our most respectable men, with a kind of brotherly affection which ought to be shown only to a gentleman of honor.

Now, Mr. President, all such mean, and more than disgraceful actions as these, are powerful auxiliaries, which work for our destruction, and which are abhorred in the sight of God and of good men.

But, sir, I cannot but bless God for the glorious anticipation of a not very distant period, when these things which now help to degrade us still no more be practiced among the sons of Africa,— for, though this, and perhaps another, generation may not experience the promised blessings of Heaven, yet, the dejected, degraded, and now enslaved children of Africa will have, in spite of all their enemies, to take their stand among the nations of the earth. And, sir, I verily believe that God has something in reserve for us, which, when he shall have poured it out upon us, will repay us for all our suffering and miseries.

APPENDIX II

On March 27, 1830, police in Charleston, South Carolina, arrested Edward Smith, a white steward on the brig Columbo *of Boston, for distributing copies of the* Appeal. *The following is Smith's confession. On May 11, the Grand Jury handed down a bill of indictment; six days later, Smith was found guilty of seditious libel, although that jury recommended clemency. On May 22, Smith was fined $1,000, and sentenced to a year in prison.*

The original transcript of Smith's confession is in State v. Edward Smith, March–May 1830, Records of Charleston County, South Carolina, Court of General Sessions, Indictments and Subpoenas, South Carolina Archives, Columbia, South Carolina. The confession also appears in William H. Pease and Jane H. Pease, "Walker's Appeal *Comes to Charleston: A Note and Documents," Journal of Negro History, 59 (1974): 287–92.*

Testimony and Confession:
Information having been rec'd by the Intendant of Charleston that a white man named Edward Smith, a Steward on board of a vessel called the Columbo recently arrived from Boston, had been Engaged in distributing some pamphlets of a very seditious & inflammatory character among the Slaves & persons of color of said City, a plan was laid for his detection and apprehension which succeeded. The Captain of the Guard by posting himself in a convenient situation for the purpose, overheard a conversation between the Said Edward Smith and a negro fellow in relation to Said Pamphlets which confirmed the Statement made to the Intendant & induced Capt'n Wesner immediately to arrest said Smith & take him to the Guard House where the Guard Committee were convened

to investigate the matter. This was on the Evening of Saturday the 27th of March 1830 & the following is the testimony adduced on the occasion

The Captain stated that the negro in the conversation above alluded to requested Smith to give him one of the Books which he had been distributing among the negroes. Smith replied that he had none left, that he had only brought out six and had given them all away. The negro then asked if he could get any more. Smith replied that he could if he went back, that those were given to him by a decent looking black man whom he believed to be a Bookseller & that he required of him that he Should give them secretly to the Black people[,] that they had some other conversation together, but that it was very much a repetition of what had been before said. One of the pamphlets in question which had been given by the negro conveying the information to the Intendant, being shewn to Smith, he said if that was the cause of his apprehension he would tell all about it & then proceeded as follows—

That the day before he left Boston, a colored man of decent appearance & very genteely dressed called on board of the vessel and asked him if he would do a favor for him. Wit[ness] replied he would if it would not bring him in trouble. The man then said that he wished him (Smith) to bring a package of pamphlets to Charleston for him and to give them to any negroes he had a mind to, or that he met, that he must do it privately and not let any white person know any thing about it. That he Wit[ness] consented & promised the man that he would do as directed. That nothing further took place between the Said man & himself, that he did not know the man who gave him the Pamphlets, that he did not know or Enquire what the pamphlets were about, but that during the passage he one day opened one of them & read a few lines when he was called away & did not look into it afterwards—(he pointed out the part of the Pamphlet which he so read, a part Embracing about two or three lines at the bottom of page — & 8 or 10 at the top of page —). From what he read he found out *that it was something in regard to the imposition upon negroes*, that when he arrived in Charleston he would not on this account have delivered the Books, if he had not pledged his word to the Boston man to do so. That after the arrival of the vessel & when the negroes came on board to discharge the Cargo, being anxious to get rid of said Pamphlets, he asked one of the negroes, if he did not want a Book or if he would have a Book & upon the Negros' replying in the affirmative he gave him one of said Pamphlets, that other negroes on board then applied to him & he gave away all that he had which were only *three* in number, that one of them was bran[d] new, another somewhat worn & the third had no cover upon it, *that the one now produced was one of the books which he had so distributed and the very one of which he had read a part on the passage,* that when he gave the books to the negroes he told them that he got them from a person in Boston, who, from his appearance, he thought was a minister. When he delivered them, the Captain & Mate were on board, but he does not know whether Either of them saw him deliver the books or heard what he said to the negroes, that during the voyage he kept the Said books at the head of his berth & when he was called away while reading one of them as above mentioned he threw it into his berth. He did not know that he was doing wrong or violating the law in distributing said books. He would know the negroes to whom he gave the books if he were again to see them. A short time after his arrival, a colored Cook or Steward was one day taken from a vessel lying near the Columbo, a black man near observed "there goes another one" to which Wit[ness] replied that it was a great Shame as it turned Every thing into Confusion on board the vessel, that the negro then rejoined that that was not half. The present is the fourth time he has been in Charleston, the third time he came, he arrived on the 22 Nov'r last & remained until the Ensuing February, that he used to come ashore at night & sometimes go to the Theatre, the first & second times he came to Charleston he did not go ashore Except to and from the Market with the Captain. He does not know why he mentioned to the negro he conversed with (see Capt'ns testimony) that he had brought six of the pamphlets with him, he brought but three.

The above is the testimony as correctly as it could be taken down. The confession of Smith was perfectly voluntary, neither the hope of reward nor the fear of punishment was held out to him as an inducement to make it. He had not been told by Capt'n Wesner that he had been arrested for circulating these pamphlets & the first intimation he had of the cause of his apprehension was when the book was produced to him & he was asked what he had done with the other five which he had said he brought with him & distributed.

His reply to this Enquiry was that if that was what he had been taken up for he would tell all about it and then went on to relate what has been above stated. He denied that he received any reward or promise of reward from the man who gave him the pamphlets and said he was to get no good from distributing them & only did it because he had pledged his word to that purpose.

The foregoing testimony & statements were made in the presence of the Intendant, Mess'rs Yates, Waring & Shand & Capt'n Wesner.

Peter J. Shand
Chairman Guard Comm'ee

SELECTED READING

Original editions of Walker's *Appeal* are extremely difficult to find. Henry Highland Garnet's reprint of the third edition, published in 1848, includes some valuable biographical information on Walker which Garnet obtained from Walker's widow. Subsequent editions include Herbert Aptheker, *One Continual Cry: David Walker's Appeal to the Colored Citizens of the World (1829–1830); Its Setting and Its Meaning* (New York, 1965), and the 1965 Hill and Wang edition, edited by Charles M. Wiltse.

The following works are among the most useful for learning more about Walker's life and times. I also wish to thank Peter Hinks, who is now the leading scholarly authority on Walker, for some helpful conversations and important suggestions regarding my introduction. Thanks, too, to Arthur Wang, who thought that the time had come for him to publish a new edition of the *Appeal*.

Clement Eaton, "A Dangerous Pamphlet in the Old South," *Journal of Southern History*, 2 (1936), 323–34.

Sylvia R. Frey, *Water from the Rock: Black Resistance in a Revolutionary Age* (Princeton, 1991).

Vincent Harding, *There Is a River: The Black Struggle for Freedom in America* (New York, 1981).

Peter P. Hinks, " 'There is a great work for you to do': The Evangelical Strategy of David Walker's *Appeal* and His Early Years in the Carolina Low Country," in Randall M. Miller and John R. McKivigan, eds., *The Moment of Decision: Biographical Essays on American Character and Regional Identity* (Westport, Conn., 1994), 99–114.

Dolan Hubbard, "David Walker's *Appeal* and the American Puritan

Jeremiadic Tradition," *The Centennial Review*, 30 (1986), 331–47.

Donald M. Jacobs, "David Walker: Boston Race Leader, 1825–1830," *Essex Institute Historical Collections*, 107 (1977), 94–107.

Donald M. Jacobs (ed.), *Courage and Conscience: Black and White Abolitionists in Boston* (Bloomington, Ind., 1993).

John Lofton, *Denmark Vesey's Revolt: The Slave Plot That Lit a Fuse to Fort Sumter* (Kent, Ohio, 1983).

William H. Pease and Jane H. Pease, "Walker's *Appeal* Comes to Charleston: A Note and Documents," *Journal of Negro History*, 59 (1974), 287–92.

Thomas G. Poole, "What Country Have I? Nineteenth-Century African-American Theological Critiques of the Nation's Birth and Destiny," *The Journal of Religion*, 72 (1992), 533–48.

Benjamin Quarles, *Black Abolitionists* (New York, 1969).

Marcus Rediker, *Between the Devil and the Deep Blue Sea: Merchant Seamen, Pirates, and the Anglo-American Maritime World, 1700–1750* (Cambridge and New York, 1987).

Sterling Stuckey, *Slave Culture: Nationalist Theory and the Foundations of Black America* (New York, 1987).

Printed in the USA
CPSIA information can be obtained
at www.ICGtesting.com
LVHW091136150724
785511LV00001B/182